EMPLOYMENT OPTIONS

EMPLOYMENT OPTIONS

The Ultimate Resource for Job Seekers
with Disabilities and other Challenges

PAULA REUBEN VIEILLET

Bartleby Press
Washington • Baltimore

Library of Congress Control Number: 2010921558
ISBN: 978-0-910-15566-3

www.MyEmploymentOptions.com

Cover Design:
Ross Feldner

Published by:
Bartleby Press
8600 Foundry Street
Mill Box 2043
Savage, MD 20763

800-953-9929
www.BartlebythePublisher.com

ACKNOWLEDGEMENTS

There were so many people who helped make this book possible.

First, thank you to my numerous clients, who bravely made the decision to go back to work. It was working with these job hunters that showed me how important it is to recognize a person's abilities, understand the process of placement and the thrill of landing a job. Their challenges inspired me to write *Disabilities / Different Abilities: A New Perspective for Job Hunters* and the accompanying *Instructor's Guide*. The book made the difference: their success was proof that my positive systematic methodology works, leading me to write this book for a broader audience.

Floyd Ballard, Instructional Designer and my professors of adult education, Dan Gardner PhD and Wayne James, PhD from the University of South Florida taught me the importance of addressing and incorporating different learning styles. I thank them for getting me started.

I want to acknowledge my parents. My father taught me how to run and maintain an honest and ethical business, and to live up to whatever challenges might arise. My mother, besides the love and caring she gave me growing up, because of her disability, helped me develop empathy and understanding of illnesses as well as how to be responsible at a young age. In addition, there was a dentist, who went the extra mile and employed my mother, even though she had a disfiguring disability. This taught me about the about the positive impact that employment can have, not only for the individual but to the family as well.

Many people have contributed with their professional knowledge in helping me to develop this material, including Ron Spitznagel, Ed.D, Professor of Rehabilitation Counseling at the University of South Florida, Charlotte Dixon, Ph.D , Chair of Rehabilitation Counseling of South Florida, Tracy Van Ess, M.A., Department of Veterans Affairs, Tom Alderhoff, PHR of APHR Associates, and Cathy Reuben, Esquire of Hirsch, Roberts, Weinstein LLP for her editing and willingness to share her legal perspective.

My professional associations, Toastmasters, International Association of Rehabilitation Professionals (IARP) and the National Employment Network Association (NENA) have taught me a lot about communicating and have provided a platform for me to express my ideas. Toastmaster and retired Air Force Staff Sergeant Jeff Thomas lent his expertise in developing the military section. Toastmaster and CEO of Happy Feet, Plus, Jane A. Strong gave me valuable feedback on the section on self-employment in addition to being a mentor. Thanks also to IARP leaders: Paul Scher, Diane Simmons-Grab, Bruce Growick, Ph.D, who opened up opportunities for me.

Thanks to my Employment Options' team who has inspired me with their suggestions, encouragement and dedication to job hunters: Flora Brehan, Ray Morrison, Derek Lewis, Suzanne Cutler, Pam Barnette, LaSheika Jones, Teresa Niers, Patricia Ferrebee, Lisa Seeley and the late Gerald Hall.

My appreciation to the leaders of the Social Security Administration's "Ticket to Work" program, the members of the Ticket to Work Advisory panel and many others who have come up with an outstanding program that truly allows people with disabilities to try to go back to work. Thanks to Phaela Kirchner for convincing me to give the ticket program a try.

My family has been very helpful throughout the writing of the book. In addition to their encouragement and love, my daughter, Sarah Vieillet helped with content on pre-employment testing and college graduates, and my son, Victor Vieillet provided amazing artistic feedback and suggestions. Michael Champlin fills our home with love, humor and music and brightens my life. He is supportive of my work and his enthusiasm is catching.

Just when I thought that I had finished this book, along came my many editors: Dan Allison, Richard Reuben, Ph.D. University of Missouri, Laura Schacter, Morgan Young and Jeremy Kay of Bartleby Press.

A special thanks to my sister, Nancy Reuben Greenfield. Nancy was my professional editor on this project, bringing many creative approaches to the material, writing important text and ultimately bringing out my very best as a writer; as an author. Her consistent belief in the mission of my work and the necessity of my methodology helped me through the tough years and continues to inspire me.

It has been my pleasure to serve people with challenges and help so many people get back to work. It is a rewarding profession that changes lives, including mine.

CONTENTS

Chapter Sixteen: Starting A New Job

PREFACE

A note to all job hunters from the author:

If you are reading this manual, either on your own or as part of a rehabilitation plan, it is because you have suffered or are likely to face difficulties in getting hired due to discrimination. Although the Americans with Disabilities Act of 1990, enforced by the Equal Employment Opportunity Commission, was created to protect you, the fact remains that discrimination is very real. Discrimination laws take many years and many individual efforts before they are truly accepted.

Just a word to let you know how important it is to stand up for your rights as a person with many different abilities and assets: Throughout history, different populations have had to fight for their right to live equally and to have equal opportunity. Slowly, through individual and group efforts, people are becoming freer to live without fear, practice their religions, vote, travel, and work without imposed barriers due to race, sex, nationality, sexual preference, age, or physical and mental abilities.

As a society, it is essential that we learn to respect each other's differences and live peacefully. All individuals have something valuable to share. Much of the progress in our workplaces has been achieved because of an individual's need for accommodations. These include flexible work schedules, computer programs that respond to vocal dictation rather than typing, and ergonomic workstations. These accommodations have improved the quality of life for many people, not only people with disabilities.

As humans we all have our strengths and weaknesses. Some people are very skilled with their hands, others are gifted with words; some are athletic, others are intellectual. Some people have been educated through the world of hard knocks, and others have pursued formal education only to find their career dreams unfulfilled or seemingly unattainable. As individuals, it is important that we develop our strengths and not allow our weaknesses or mistakes to rule our lives.

Sometimes it feels as though our only option has been taken away; however, no matter how real that feels, there is still something special about you that can be developed and shared. Your most important contribution may be in your future.

In this manual, I challenge you to focus on your strengths, to understand, accept, and accommodate your weaknesses, and to learn techniques to make this journey a little easier and more fruitful. No matter what your situation, I urge you to stand up for your right to equality, the right to be human, the right to dignity, and the right to equal access to employment.
Best wishes,

Paula

Attention Job Hunters!

This book will help you:

➜ Establish realistic job goals

➜ Get interviews over the phone

➜ Talk about your abilities

➜ Increase your self-esteem

➜ Become confident in your job search

➜ Develop a career change resume

➜ Explain gaps in your employment

➜ Handle applications and interviews using protected rights under the Americans with Disabilities Act

➜ Become an effective job hunter

➜ Get the job you really deserve

He who knows others is wise. He who knows himself is enlightened.
—Lao Tzu

WHAT TYPE OF JOB HUNTER ARE YOU?

Attention Job Hunters!

You can be a great employee, but a lousy job hunter.

Starting and managing your job search is challenging — even for the most sophisticated job hunter.

This step-by-step, sure-proof method for job search and job change will make it easier for you to get hired in a job that is just right for you.

What Type of Job Hunter Are You?

❑ Student

❑ Homemaker

❑ Military

❑ Professional

❑ Blue Collar

❑ Unemployed

❑ Career Changer

❑ Downsized

❑ Senior

❑ Workers' Compensation

❑ Disabled

What Type of Job Hunter Are You?

	Yes	Somewhat	No
1. I am currently employed.	_____	_____	_____
2. I have been job hunting for less than 30 days.	_____	_____	_____
3. I have been job hunting for 3-6 months.	_____	_____	_____
4. I have been job hunting for over 6 months.	_____	_____	_____
5. I enjoy my line of work, yet I am dissatisfied with my company.	_____	_____	_____
6. I have been sending out my resume without much response.	_____	_____	_____
7. I am familiar with the Equal Opportunity Employment laws and what is legally admissible for an employer to ask in an interview.	_____	_____	_____
8. I know where to look for jobs in my line of work.	_____	_____	_____
9. I have a career plan.	_____	_____	_____
10. I know that there is a better position for me, if someone only knew about me.	_____	_____	_____

	Yes	Somewhat	No
11. I have just returned from military duty and I am unsure where I fit in the civilian world.	____	____	____
12. I feel like I would be able to advance if I had more training or education.	____	____	____
13. I have a disability which makes it difficult to find employment.	____	____	____
14. I like job hunting.	____	____	____
15. I am comfortable using the computer.	____	____	____
16. I fill out lots of job applications but never hear back from the employer.	____	____	____
17. I feel that I am overqualified for my current position.	____	____	____
18. I feel like I use my degree in my work.	____	____	____
19. I want to work, but I am worried about being successful in the workplace.	____	____	____
20. I have a good idea what other people in my profession are earning.	____	____	____
21. I have time to research companies.	____	____	____

22. I feel comfortable telephoning
prospective employers and inquiring
about job duties and job requirements.   _____   _____   _____

23. I feel like I am paid less than what I
am worth.   _____   _____   _____

24. I usually do well at interviews.   _____   _____   _____

25. I have a good idea of what kind of job
would best suit me.   _____   _____   _____

26. I am having difficulties in
explaining my gaps in employment.   _____   _____   _____

27. I am having or have had problems
with my supervisor.   _____   _____   _____

28. I am worried about getting
a bad reference from my previous
employer.   _____   _____   _____

29. I have defined job goals.   _____   _____   _____

30. Since I lost my job, I am having trouble
with feeling good about myself.   _____   _____   _____

31. I have difficulty getting along with my
co-workers.

   _____   _____   _____

32. I am good at negotiating salary.

   _____   _____   _____

33. I am familiar with employment agencies.

   _____   _____   _____

34. I stopped working to raise my children
or to care for parents.

   _____   _____   _____

35. I have a service related disability.

   _____   _____   _____

36. I often panic when I am confined to small
areas.

   _____   _____   _____

37. I have nightmares frequently about my
military or work-related trauma.

   _____   _____   _____

38. I have never really had a steady job.

   _____   _____   _____

39. I just graduated from school and
all the employers that I talked to
want work experience.

   _____   _____   _____

40. I am comfortable following up with
employers after a job interview.

   _____   _____   _____

	Yes	Somewhat	No

41. I am comfortable talking to people about their work. _____ _____ _____

42. I hate asking people if their company is hiring. _____ _____ _____

43. I am an active volunteer. _____ _____ _____

44. I enjoy interviewing. _____ _____ _____

EDUCATIONAL LEVEL

Place an X in front of the appropriate level   **Year Completed/Course of Study**

	Less than High School	
	High School or GED	
	College Degree	
	Master's Degree	
	Doctorate Degree	
	Professional Licensures	

Place an X in the appropriate grids.

Annual Salary	Below $14,000	Between $14,000-$18,000	Between $18,000-$29,000	Between $29,000-$45,000	Between $46,000-$80,000	Between $80,000-$100,00	Between $100,000-$200,000
Actual or Prior							
Desired Salary							

If you answered yes to questions 4, 26, or 30, you must be emotionally exhausted. Chapters Three and Four will help you identify your feelings and learn coping strategies that will help you through these difficult times. The section on *Coping With Job-Search Stress* will be of particular value to you. Work through the exercises on pages 35 and 257–259 thoroughly and practice every day. You will start feeling better.

If you answered yes to questions, 4, 6, 13, 16, or no to question 7, you are probably using red flag words that may be scaring potential employers. Pay special attention to Chapter 9, *Facing the Job Market*. It is essential that you learn about your rights as a job hunter. Even though you may be facing discrimination, it does not have to be that way.

Questions 9, 25, and 29 refer to job goals and career direction. If you are unsure or responded no to these questions you are probably having trouble with your job search. It is much easier to find a job if you know what you are looking for. It is important that you get to know yourself, your skills, interests, strengths, and abilities better. The section *Getting to Know You* will help quite a bit. Depending upon your particular circumstances or challenges, you may get some ideas from the menus of jobs for students and transitioning military or from the alternative job section for the physically and emotionally challenged.

Answering yes to question 17, 26 or 28 indicates that you may be worrying about something that can easily be addressed in an interview, a resume, or even on a job application. You will benefit from studying the section *On Your Mark, Get Set, Go,* which is all about how to present yourself to prospective employers in a way that your strengths and qualifications are more strongly highlighted than your obstacles.

If you answered yes to questions 12 or 23, if your educational level is high school or less, or if your salary level is below $18,000 annually, then furthering your education may be of benefit to you. Check out Chapter 8 on going back to school.

If you answered yes to questions 3, 4, 6, 10 or no to question 22, you need to develop a strong plan for your job search before you get too discouraged. Brushing up on your job search methods and career exploration techniques will be of great benefit to you. Pay special attention to Chapters 10, 11, and 12. One of the most effective and under-utilized job search tools is the telephone. Telephone skills are not that hard to learn, and you will be glad that you made the extra effort.

If you answered no to questions 8, 14, or 20, you are lacking some basic information that will make your job search a lot more fun and fruitful. Labor market information is easy to obtain and will make a world of difference in how you approach your job search. Check out Chapter 10.

You are a well-adjusted job hunter if you answered yes to questions 8, 20, or 32, or if you are earning comparably to what you want to make, and you have a good idea of your value to a prospective employer. Although you may not be in the job of your dreams, chances are you will make a fairly good impression in interviews. If you are having difficulty in finding a job despite of your clear-cut sense of direction, it may be that your career field is in serious decline or that there are a lot of job hunters with your qualifications. In other words, you have some competition! Not to worry, though: a refined job goal, improved interviewing skills, and a top notch resume can bring you up to the next level: a job offer.

Question 15 refers to computer skills. Not all jobs require computer skills, but many companies use computer programs to screen applicants or to list job openings. Even if you are never going to be a whiz on computers, some very basic skills will help out. In the section on *Getting Help with Challenges* (Chapter 4), you will find information on where and how to get help.

Questions 27, 28, 31, and 38 refer to interpersonal relations on-the-job. If you marked yes to these questions, you may be working for an unreasonable employer or you may be experiencing difficulties because of a hidden disability. Check out the section on *Hidden Challenges* (Chapter 5). The solution to your problems may be a lot easier than you think.

For questions 11, 35, 36, and 37, you may be suffering from post-traumatic stress. People who have suffered severe trauma in battle, at work, or in their personal lives may have an increased sensitivity and react strongly in certain situations. See page 83.

If you answered yes to question 4, 26, and 34 you can learn how to present your time off (for example, with your children) as a positive attribute.

If you answered yes to question 28, while it is not always possible to change what might have happened on a previous job, concerns about poor references are one of the easiest problems to address in a job search. See pages 176–179.

If your answer is yes to question 39, you need work experience. Find out where to get work experience on pages 159–161.

If you feel like you need more education than what you currently possess, the chapter on *Getting Help with Challenges* has information about getting into school, going backing to school and how to pay for your education.

Now that you know more about your
challenges as a job hunter, it is time to get to know you
and to determine the job goal
that is just right for you.

GETTING TO KNOW YOU...

> This chapter will help you through the initial process of identifying your workplace preferences and values.
>
> Each one of us has individual preferences and strengths. The more self-awareness we possess, the better we are able to communicate this information in a job interview.
>
> It will be easy to answer some of the items, while others may require a little thought or may not have a clear-cut response.
>
> This is okay.
>
> Enjoy the process. You are heading in a new direction...

Identifying the right job goal means knowing
what is important to you, what is special about you,
and matching your profile to a job that complements you.

What Interests You?

(Check all that apply)

People tend to gravitate to types of jobs that express their personal interests. Identifying your basic interests gives you insight into your personality and can help guide your career direction.

☐ Mechanics

☐ Science

☐ Investigating

☐ Helping People

☐ Technology

☐ Sales

☐ Managing People

☐ Clerical Tasks

☐ Mathematics

☐ Reading

☐ Writing

☐ Sketching

☐ Decorating

☐ Cooking

☐ Sports

☐ Movies

☐ Fashion

☐ Indoor Activities

☐ Driving

☐ Building Things

☐ Gardening

☐ Home Maintenance

☐ Music

☐ Shopping

☐ Animals

☐ Religious Activities

☐ Traveling

☐ Fine Dining

☐ Theater

☐ Working Out

☐ Children

☐ Senior Citizens

☐ Parties

☐ Outdoor Activities

☐ _____

☐ _____

What Is Your Ideal Work Environment?
(Check your preferences)

Take a minute to think about what kind of job and company environment you prefer. Knowing your preferences can help bring your dream one step closer. There are no right or wrong answers. Some people prefer working "graveyard" shifts; others are only happy working "nine-to-five."

❑ Small company

   ❑ Large organization

      ❑ Inside work

         ❑ Outside work

            ❑ Job with traveling

               ❑ Stationary position

                  ❑ Routine work

                     ❑ Varied work duties

                        ❑ Frequent interaction with people

                           ❑ Little interaction with people

                             ❑ Wear business clothes

                                ❑ Wear jeans

                                   ❑ Wear a uniform

                                      ❐ First shift

                                      ❐ Second Shift

                                      ❐ Third Shift

                                      ❐ Weekends

Knowing Your Strengths

(Choose seven words from the following list which best describe you.)

Alert	Attentive	Committed
Capable	Common sense	Confident
Courteous	Cooperative	Creative
Competent	Consistent	Cultured
Dependable	Detail-oriented	Diplomatic
Effective	Efficient	Energetic
Empathetic	Enthusiastic	Fast learner
Good listener	Innovative	Honest
Hard-working	Loyal	Cheerful
Imaginative	Genuine	Punctual
Independent	Motivated	Mature
Orderly	Objective	Organized
Outgoing	Professional	Productive
Persistent	Poised	Perceptive
Patient	Responsible	Sincere
Positive attitude	Stable	Trustworthy

My Strengths

1.

2.

3.

4.

5.

6.

7.

Some people with challenges are able to talk in detail about their weaknesses, yet have more difficulty describing their strengths. The ability to verbalize your strengths is crucial in a job interview.

What Makes You the Person For the Job?

(Fill in the blanks using your seven strength words from the previous page.)

1. An employer would benefit from hiring me because I am _____ and I can perform this type of work well.

2. You can count on me because I am _____.

3. Employers appreciate my ability to be _____.

4. I have always been _____ in my work.

5. My co-workers appreciate the fact that I am _____.

6. In my previous job, I was very _____, which was just what my employer needed.

7. I think it would be in your best interest to hire me because I am _____, and this is a very important quality in this job.

Your Personality

Your personality "types" influences the types of jobs where you would feel most comfortable.

Circle those personality traits that you feel are most like you (or that friends would use to describe you).

Personalities can be classified as:

❏ **Out-going** - Loves to be around people and meet new people

❏ **Introvert** - Looks inward and prefers activities alone

❏ **Perceptive** - Can easily pick up on peoples' personalities or needs

❏ **Sensitive** - Easily affected by environment

❏ **Passive** - Prefers to let others make decisions

❏ **Dominant** - Prefers to be the decision-maker and influence others

❏ **Affiliations** - A need to form friendships and attachments

❏ **Accepting** - Able to go with the flow and accept change easily

❏ **Critical** - Inclined to judge and perceive imperfections

❏ **Spontaneous** - Makes plans at spur of moment

❏ **Planful** - Prefers to plan activities

❏ **Safe** - People tend to feel safe around you and open up easily

❏ **Protective** - Feels a responsibility for the well-being and safety of others

❏ **Calm** - Able to handle most situations without feeling nervousness

❏ **Serious** - Approaches responsibilities with deep concern

❏ **Enthusiastic** - A tendency to see the bright side and tell others

_____

_____

Use the words circled from the previous page to describe your personality.

How would your friends and family describe you?

How would your co-workers describe you?

Did your personality negatively affect you in a previous job, or did it enhance your performance?

What types of personalities make you feel the most comfortable?

While personality alone will not qualify you for most jobs, personality *can* be a factor in how well you do in a particular job, with a certain company, or in an interview situation.

What Do I Really Need From My Job?

High salary	Convenient working hours
Flexible schedule	Non-stressful work
Stable employment	Benefits
Meaningful work	Room for growth
Great co-workers	Advancement within company
Challenging work	Immediate employment
Learn new skills	Other

Pick four of the following phrases and list them in order of importance to you.

Current Goals	Five-Year Goals
1.	1.
2.	2.
3.	3.
4.	4.

Your Abilities

One of the keys to finding the right career is to identify and acknowledge the things you do well. These are your abilities:

Rate your Abilities - *Put an S for Superior, E for Excellent and, A for Average.*

_____**Physical Strength**
The ability to work in all climates, lift heavy objects, and sustain strenuous activity. Important in trades, outdoor jobs, military, police, and firefighting.

_____**Motor Coordination**
The ability to precisely control your body and perform certain tasks. Important for athletics, cooks, musicians, machine operators, and dancers.

_____**Hand-Eye Coordination**
The ability to use hands in a precise fashion to perform detailed tasks with hands. Needed for assembly, welding, fine art, surgeons, dentists, computer design, and some trades.

_____**Mechanical Ability**
Understanding of mechanical principles. Needed for mechanics, sciences, engineering, computer programming, medicine, and sciences.

_____**Social Abilities**
The ability to relate to people, explain things to others, and make people feel at ease. Essential for sales, public relations, counseling, human resources, nursing, and education.

_____**Routine Work**
The ability to do repetitive and/or similar work on a daily basis. Examples are housekeeping, factory work, or stocking.

_____**Writing Ability**
The ability to convey information in a written format. Important in jobs requiring written communications like writers, editors, attorneys, business managers and marketing professionals.

_____**Leadership Ability**
Ability to lead people. Most professions look for leaders, especially for jobs in management, politics, education, non-profit companies, and business.

_____**Multi-Tasking**
Useful in hospitality industries, clerical work, case management, and nursing.

_____**Spatial Ability**
The ability to visualize or think in three dimensions, and picture objects from a diagram or sketch. Useful for jobs in reading blueprints, arts, sciences, and technical fields.

_____**Verbal Ability**
The ability to speak with ease and convey ideas or facts.

_____**Math Ability**
The ability to calculate and use mathematical formulas and principles. Important in medicine, technology, science, engineering, higher level trades, business, and some clerical fields.

_____**Artistic Ability**
The ability to express creatively feelings and ideas through the arts.

_____**Numerical Reasoning**
The ability to reason with and use numbers and work with quantitative material and ideas.

_____**Verbal Reasoning**
The ability to reason with words, and to understand and use concepts expressed in words.

_____**Auditory Reasoning**
The ability to use judgment and common reason when listening to others.

_____**Crystallized Thinking**
The ability to use your knowledge of words and their meanings to generate ideas.

_____**Fluid Thinking**
The ability to solve new problems by perceiving relationships and completing analogies.

> Your chances for success and advancement
> in a career field
> largely depend upon
> your ability to do the job.

*List those abilities from page 22 that have an S or E next to them
as well as any other abilities that you may have.*

1. _____

2. _____

3. _____

4. _____

5. _____

6. _____

7. _____

8. _____

9. _____

10. _____

Embrace your abilities. Strengthen those abilities.

> Employers hire people who <u>are able</u> to get the job done.

Please note: A number of excellent aptitude tests measure specific abilities. Standardized testing can be quite helpful in quantifying your abilities. You may have superior abilities in areas that you never realized. See the Resource section for information on Aptitude Testing.

Summing Up Your Work Preferences

Look at the previous pages and record your findings.

Interests	
Work Environment	
Strengths	
Personality	
Needs	
Abilities	

The nice thing about just being you is that different jobs require different abilities.

A FRESH START

Whether you are just starting to work, wanting to change careers, or changing jobs due to circumstances beyond your control, your feelings and attitudes will affect your ability to get and keep a job.

Any job loss, whether anticipated or not, can trigger feelings. Learning to accept the situation, no matter how painful it feels or how unfairly your were treated, will help you to move on.

The first step to your new job is to identify and acknowledge your feelings and thoughts about your work situation.

Remember, these are just feelings, words, and thoughts.

A Fresh Start...

Employment Options

Starting Out

Common feelings and attitudes of job hunters who are just starting out or changing careers:

Doubt

I am not sure if I would be good at this job.
Will I like this kind of work?

Fear

I am not sure I want to do this my whole life.
I can never possibly live off these wages the rest of my life.
How long will it take me to find a job?

Panic

What if I get fired?
What if no one wants to hire me?

Most people do not know exactly what they want to do when they are first entering the workplace or when changing careers.

It is difficult to know how marketable your skills are or where you would best fit in if you have worked in the same job for many years or have never worked.

A job is not a "life sentence." It is a stopping point that may be short or long-term.

Job Change

**Did you know that few people stay in the same job
or with the same company their whole lives?**

> The average American changes jobs seven times in his or her lifetime.

A person's job changes for many reasons:

BUSINESS ISSUES:

> Decline in company business
>
> Budget cuts
>
> Restructuring of company
>
> Technology upgrades
>
> Outsourcing
>
> Company moves
>
> Change in personal needs (such as benefits or schedule change)
>
> Completion of education

UNFORSEEABLE EVENTS:

> Off-the-job accident or illness
>
> Family illness or death
>
> On-the-job accident
>
> Sickness
>
> Stock market crash
>
> 9-11 or other acts of violence

CIRCUMSTANCES:

> Need different hours
>
> Completed education
>
> Need higher salary
>
> Need more or different benefits
>
> Need work that is a better fit

Job Loss

When you lose your job due to termination, illness, injury, or downsizing, it is different than making a job change by choice.

Below are listed common initial reactions after losing a job.

Circle the feelings that apply to you:

Shock
What??!
Not me!

Denial
It is not true.
Someone must have made a mistake.

Numbness
An inability to feel.
I just can't talk about it.

Panic
What if I cannot find another job?
How am I going to pay my bills?

These feelings are natural and temporary.

It is just part of how it feels to lose a job.

Being downsized, terminated, unemployed, under-employed, being in a poor job fit, and looking for a job during a time of high unemployment are all stressful situations. They bring to the surface a whole range of strong and powerful emotions.

Circle the feelings that apply to you:

Anxiety

What will my family say?
How will I pay my bills?
What will I do?

Anger

How could they?
I'll get them back for this.

Shame

How am I going to tell everyone?
What if someone finds out?

Blame

If they had listened to me, this would have never happened.
You should have never let me take this job.
It is all their fault.
They should never have let us work under those conditions.

Sadness

I really liked what I did.
I miss everybody.

Having unpleasant feelings is part of being human
and a natural response to job stress.

Being out of a job and looking for work can lead to false perceptions about you and your situation.

Circle the feelings that apply to you:

Over-Generalization

Bad things always happen to me.
Nobody cares about me.
I will never get better.
I'm a failure at everything.

Guilt

I should have seen it coming.
I never should have accepted that project.
I should have said something.

Avoidance

I'm fine.
Let's have a drink.
I am not feeling well.
Let's talk about something else.

Self-Pity

It never fails.
No one will hire someone with a disability.
No one will hire someone in their 40s or 50s.
I'm too old to start over.

Depression

Why even try to look for a job?
What difference will it make?
I might as well give up.
I'm no good for anything.

Please note: If destructive thoughts do not go away, professional help may be indicated. Consult your family doctor or a mental health professional. Trauma can trigger a physical state of fight or flight that affects your health, causing a physically depressed state. Depression is a treatable disease.

You **cannot** *change the past.*

No matter how much you are hurting,
negativity can keep you
from getting the job you really want.

Holding on to negative thoughts
Only Hurts You!

When you change your thoughts,
your feelings and attitudes
will begin to change.

Changing the way you think

will change the way you interview.

Managing Your Thoughts

> **Try replacing your negative thoughts with helpful thoughts.**

Circle your new ways of thinking.

Forgiveness

I did the best I could.

It was an accident.

They did the best they could.

I made a mistake.

Acceptance

The company took a different direction than I was going.

I got injured.

I can no longer do this kind of work.

Things change.

The competition had a better product.

It really had nothing to do with me, it is just business.

Reconciliation

The company was losing money and had to cut back.

It is more difficult to remain competitive in a global market.

The boss just is not capable of being there for me.

The industry I work in has it's ups and downs.

Feelings and thoughts are closely aligned. Looking at a situation differently can help you cope with the natural feelings that arise after job loss. At first, managing your thoughts to make them more positive will seem awkward. With practice though, thinking positively about your new situation will become more natural.

New Opportunities

I have always wanted to go back to school.

I am busy exploring new directions.

I have always wanted to be a _____.

I am excited about the opportunity to learn something new.

Positive Thinking

My challenges have made me stronger.

I have a lot of good qualities.

I have always tried my hardest.

Something good is coming my way.

I am a stable and loyal employee.

Some employer will be lucky to get me.

I know there is a job out there me; it is just a matter of finding it.

I deserve a job I truly enjoy.

Accepting Your Feelings

Complete the following sentences to help you accept your feelings.

1. I am excited about the opportunity to _____.

2. Just for today, I will try not to _____.

3. Everyday I am getting better and better at _____.

4. I am proud of myself for _____.

5. I enjoy learning about _____.

6. Today, I am feeling good about_____.

7. Even though I am not employed, I am busy _____.

8. I am happy that_____.

9. I have the opportunity to _____.

10. I can _____.

If you are like most Americans, you have a tendency to link your self-esteem to your ability to obtain and maintain employment. In other words, you measure your worth mostly by what you do to earn money.

While it is true that being without employment may be a hardship, especially when you have bills to pay, your value as a person is certainly more than your value as "just a bread winner." You are a valuable person whether or not you have a job.

You probably know people who are not working who you still admire and value. Perhaps you have a favorite grandma or a ten-year-old son who you adore. What about your retired neighbors, perhaps the ones who watch your dog when you are away? A person, you see, is much more than just a job.

Positive thinking creates a positive attitude.

Employers hire positive people.

You are more than just a job!!!

Sense of Connectedness
Spiritual Well Being
Purposeful Intellect

Money

Work

Family
Hobbies
Music
Prayer
Sports

Friends
Helping Others
Volunteering

Creativity
Character
Childhood
Beliefs
Education
Heritage
Integrity
Skills
Values
Work History

Transportation

Health

Safety

Food
Shelter

Finding Your Balance

Many Americans (especially males) link their self-esteem to their work. Without work, some people feel worthless. Work, however, is only one part of your life. This exercise is designed to help you recover and recognize your self-esteem.

Circle the phrases that describe the areas in your life that currently provide you with joy and satisfaction.

Your Head: Describe yourself in positive terms.
- Sense of Connectedness
- Spiritual Well-Being
- Purposeful Intellect
- Positive Attitude

Your Shoulders: Which responsibilities are you managing well?
- Money
- Work
- Credit Cards
- Bankruptcy
- Family
- School

Your Arms: Where do you reach out and connect with others?
- Friends
- Family
- Volunteering
- Helping Others
- Prayer
- Sports
- Hobbies
- Music

Your Body: Describe three positive values that best characterize you.
- Character
- Beliefs
- Heritage
- Skills
- Work History
- Childhood
- Integrity

Your Legs: Are you able to get around?
- Health
- Transportation

Your Feet: Are your most basic needs being met?
- Safety
- Food
- Housing

VOCATIONAL CHALLENGES

Many factors may make it difficult for a person to find a job. Some challenges are personal. Others are universal. Some people have visible challenges, and others have hidden challenges.

Just because you have a vocational challenge does not mean that you will never find a job.

Once you can identify your special challenges, you will better be able to accommodate those challenges and find the job that will work for you.

What Are Your Particular Challenges?

❑ Lay-Off   ❑ Returning Military

❑ Emotional Challenges   ❑ Poor Credit

❑ Over-Qualified   ❑ Need Retraining

❑ Physical Challenges   ❑ Fired From Job

❑ Highly Specialized Field   ❑ Need a Job Change

❑ Unstable Work History   ❑ No Child Care

❑ Gaps in Employment   ❑ Low Self-Esteem

❑ Criminal History   ❑ New Graduate

❑ Limited Education   ❑ No Transportation

❑ Learning Disabilities   ❑ Never Worked

❑ Seniors   ❑ Poor Job Market

❑ Poor References   ❑ Unsafe Living Conditions

It can be very difficult to overcome your challenges
all by yourself.

Getting help with challenges is a positive step
towards your new job.

Challenges	Help with Challenges
❏ **Anxiety** ❏ **Depression** → Are you often feeling sad? → Do you have a hard time getting out of bed? → Do you feel overwhelmed by your problems? → Do you worry a lot? → Do you feel fearful, especially in new situations? → Do your moods keep you from doing things that are good for you? → Do you often feel guilty?	Call 911 for emergencies **Join a support group for job hunters in your community:** ❏ Check out your local job service or unemployment office for job search or job hunter's support groups and for information on job-seeking skills training programs. ❏ Contact your church or synagogue for information about support groups. **Mental Health Counseling:** ❏ Call your insurance company for a list of providers. ❏ Talk to your Employee Assistance Program—EAP—at work for assistance in accessing appropriate services. ❏ Look in the Yellow Pages for the names of private and public mental health counselors. Many non-profits have sliding fee scales. ❏ Talk to family doctor or psychiatrist to screen for physical illnesses that affect your mood. ❏ Seek out a member of the clergy.
❏ **Financial/Poor Credit** → Are collectors calling you? → Do you have more debt than you can manage?	❏ Poor credit or recent bankruptcy may keep you from being hired at banks, credit card companies, and other customer service jobs that involve money transactions. ❏ Consolidate your credit cards. ❏ Obtain credit reports from: Equifax—**www.equifax.com** Experion—**www.experion.com** TransUnion—**www.transunion.com** Work with each creditor individually to clean up your credit. Most credit card companies will agree to a reduced cash settlement of very high balances as a way to help you avoid bankruptcy.

The Americans with Disabilities Act, a federal law, requires that communities provide transportation for persons unable to physically access public transportation.

Contact your city hall or bus company for more information. A doctor's note will probably be required to document your degree of disability and your need for transportation accommodations.

Challenges	Help with Challenges
❑ **Transportation** ➜ Are you unable to drive? ➜ Are you without a car? ➜ Are you having trouble getting to work because of a disability? ➜ Do you need help with arranging transportation?	❑ Call your local bus and taxi companies. Talk to their ADA coordinator or transportation coordinator to find out about programs designed to help disabled individuals with transportation. (You may need to provide a letter or form from your doctor to qualify for special transportation.) ❑ Ask the bus company if it has a share-a-ride program that allows you to take your bicycle on the bus. ❑ Call your city government to find out about different transportation programs including share-a-ride programs commuter programs and transportation for disabled persons. ❑ Centers for Independent Living are a great help in assisting qualified individuals with disabilities secure services including bus passes and special transportation. They also provide other services designed to help persons live independently, including referral services, home modification, advocacy, and interpreters. Look in the White Pages of your phone directory for local contact information, or see a list of centers (by state) at: **www.abledata.com**
❑ **Safety** ➜ Are you living in an abusive situation? ➜ Do you fear for your life or safety? ➜ Is your spouse, boyfriend, or girlfriend hurting you?	❑ Call the police – call 911 – if you are in immediate danger. ❑ Get a restraining order from your local judge. ❑ Shelters may be available to provide you and your children with safe housing where your abusive partner will be unable to find you. ❑ Change of housing—consider moving in with your parents, brothers, sisters or friends until you are out of danger.

Job hunters face many types of challenges.

Challenges	Help with Challenges
❐ **Shelter** ➜ Do you need help finding suitable housing? ➜ Are you unable to afford safe housing on your current income?	❐ Goodwill, the Salvation Army, homeless shelters, drug and alcohol treatment centers, churches, family, and friends may be able to provide temporary assistance with shelter. ❐ HUD - Housing Authority Program provides low-income persons, seniors, veterans, native Americans, and persons with disabilities access to affordable housing through subsidized rent and home ownership programs. Visit **www.hud.gov** for more information.
❐ **Isolation** ➜ Are you feeling lonely? ➜ Are you isolated?	❐ Call your friends, family, or support group members. A phone call can help bring you closer together. ❐ Churches - Synagogues - Mosque. ❐ Consider living in a group home or halfway house. ❐ Take a class or pursue a hobby. ❐ Get a pet.
❐ **Criminal Record** ➜ Have you been convicted of a felony? ➜ Are you having trouble finding work because of a criminal record?	❐ Each state has its own rules for restoring rights to convicted felons. ❐ Contact criminal rights organizations in your state to see if you can get your record expunged or sealed. ❐ Be sure to carefully read the job application. Many companies only go back seven or ten years on a criminal background check. ❐ Public record laws vary widely from state to state. Some states release criminal records to the public. Others do not. ❐ You may need a new job goal that fits your circumstance better.

Challenges	Help with Challenges
☐ **Seniors** ➜ Are you over the age of 55? ➜ Are you currently living below the poverty level?	☐ **Seniors** Many cities and counties have programs for senior workers such as the Green Thumb Program and Senior Works. These programs often pay minimum wage, and the work is usually part-time. There are usually some income restrictions. The American Association of Retired Persons (AARP) also has work programs designed to meet the needs of senior workers.
☐ **Military** ➜ Did you serve in the military? ➜ Do you have a military service related disability?	☐ **US Department of Veterans** Provides medical, rehabilitation, and vocational services for qualified veterans nationwide at medical centers and veterans affairs offices.
☐ **Vocational Assistance** ➜ Are you having problems interviewing for jobs? ➜ Do you need help with your job search?	☐ **One-Stop Centers** This federal government program works with the general public throughout the United States. At One-Stop Centers a person can use the computer system to research and apply for local, state, and federal jobs. You can also get information on government retraining programs and speak with a job counselor. To find the center nearest where you live call **1-877-US-2JOBS** or TTY **1-877-889-5627** or go to **www.servicelocator.org**

Challenges	Help with Challenges
❒ **Medical and Vocational Assistance** ➜ Are you having physical or emotional problems that are keeping you from working? ➜ Are you unable to get the health care that you need? ➜ Would you like to talk with a professional about your particular circumstances?	❒ **State Vocational Rehabilitation** This agency works directly with people with disabilities and illnesses that interfere with a person's ability to return to work. They may be able to help with obtaining appropriate medical and/or psychological treatment as well as vocational assistance. Search the web for your state's vocational rehabilitation services or look in your telephone directory under state agencies. ❒ **Health/Dental/Mental Health** Many communities have doctors and other medical professional who volunteer their time for persons unable to pay for medical services. By dialing 211, you can obtain telephone numbers for local resources. ❒ **Non-Profit Agencies** An organization that doesn't have a goal to make a profit. It may be entirely funded by voluntary donations or government grants. ❒ **Public Health Departments** Offer some free or low-cost medical and dental treatment. They provide diagnosis and treatment of communicable diseases such as AIDS, sexually transmitted diseases, and tuberculosis.
❒ **Workers' Compensation** ➜ Are you currently receiving worker's compensation? ➜ Did you have a car accident that left you unable to work? ➜ Do you have an illness or disability covered by long-term or short-term disability insurance?	❒ **Division of Workers' Compensation** Each state has its own rules and regulations. Their services are targeted to assist and educate persons injured on-the-job regarding their rights and options. ❒ **Insurance Companies** Persons on long-term or short-term disability can ask for a vocational evaluation to help them develop a "return-to-work plan." It may be worthwhile to suggest this to your insurance carrier if it has increased your liability because you are not working.

Challenges	Help with Challenges
☐ **Vocational Assistance** ➜ Do you receive SSI or SSDI and want to try returning to work? *Talk to your Social Security Work Incentive Liaison about your individual case as benefits may differ depending on your particular situation.	☐ **Social Security Ticket to Work** The federally sponsored Ticket to Work program allows a disabled person receiving Social Security Income (SSI) or Social Security Disability Insurance (SSDI) to return to work with no fear of losing Social Security benefits. This is a completely voluntary program with no risks for the job hunter. Job hunters benefit from a trial work period that lasts from 9 to 12 months. During this time a person continues to receive cash benefits from the Social Security Administration* as well as income from work. The extra money can be used to help you catch up on bills. Ticket to Work participants continue to receive health benefits from Medicare or Medicaid for 8 1/2 years after the trial work period.* They are exempt from medical reviews during the time that the ticket is assigned to an Employment Network. Those who return to full-time employment but are unable to maintain employment may reinstate their Social Security benefits without having to reapply. Many private and non-profit agencies are registered Ticket to Work Employment Networks (ENs), including Employment Options: **www.MyEmploymentOptions.com** It is the EN's job to follow-up with you for a six-year period. During this time the EN continues to assist you with any work-related issues that may arise, such as changing jobs, negotiating reasonable accommodations, getting along with co-workers, etc. A list of all ENs can be found on the web site **www.yourtickettowork.com** ENs have the right to turn you down for services if they do not feel that you are a good candidate for their company. Ticket to Work is a performance-based retention program, which means that the EN who works with you gets paid only if you go back to work and keep working.

Challenges	Help with Challenges
Private Vocational Evaluators and Career Counselors ➜ Do you need help in determining appropriate job goals? ➜ Are you interested in vocational testing? ➜ Are you having trouble finding out if your retraining goals will lead to employment? ➜ Do you know what to expect from a vocational evaluator or career counselor?	▶ Understanding and experience with vocational testing. ▶ Knowledge of the local labor market. ▶ Experience in assisting persons with challenges return to work. ▶ Counseling or human resource ▶ Many have job placement specialties. ▶ Many have experience with your particular challenge. ▶ Many offer training. ▶ Most have local job placement experience.
❏ **Where would I find a private vocational evaluator or career counselor?**	▶ Certified Rehabilitation Counselors, **http://ncra-net.org** ▶ International Association of Rehabilitation Counselors, **www.rehabpro.org** ▶ **www.MyEmploymentOptions.com**
❏ **What about career counseling on the Internet?**	While some of the career profile tests might provide some insight, a trained vocational evaluator correlates career testing with an in-depth vocational interview and together they provide the best picture of your career potential. Without a personal interview the results of a career assessment is comparable to a doctor making a diagnosis based on test results alone.

Challenges	Help with Challenges
EDUCATION ☐ **No High School Diploma** ➜ Were you unable to finish high school even though you made good grades?	▶ **General Educational Development (GED) Testing Service:** For people who did not finish high school, the GED exam is required for most vocational training programs and colleges. The GED is considered the equivalent of a high school diploma. Local testing centers in the U.S. and Canada can be located by calling their toll-free hotline at (800) 626-9433. For more information go to the American Council on Education website at: **www.acenet.edu**
☐ **No College Diploma** ➜ Did you start college but never finish? ➜ Would college help you in your career? ➜ Are your test scores high enough to qualify you for admission into the college of your choice?	**Most vocational training programs and colleges have admission requirements.** One or more tests or assessment tools may be required; schools want students with the knowledge and ability to succeed in their programs. ▶ **TABE** - The Test of Adult Basic Education^{tm} (CTB:McGraw-Hill) assesses basic reading, math, and language skills. TABE is used by many vocational schools to determine admissions eligibility.
☐ **Getting into College** ➜ Would you qualify for admission into a university or technical school?	▶ **ACT**^{tm} - A widely accepted college entrance exam, the ACT Assessment® is designed to assess high school students' general educational development and their ability to complete college-level work. The tests cover four skill areas: English, mathematics, reading, and science. For more information or to register go to: **www.act.org** ▶ **SAT**^{tm} - The SAT is another widely accepted test. It measures verbal and mathematical reasoning skills students have developed over time and need for academic success. For more information or to register go to: **www.collegeboard.com**

Challenges	Help with Challenges
EDUCATION ❐ **College Credit for Life Experiences** ➜ Do you have a lot of work experience and knowledge in a certain field, but you lack the formal education to get promoted or increase your earnings?	▶ AP- You may take Advanced Placement or CLEP (The College-Level Examination Program®) tests to get credit for college subjects that you may have studied on your own or in high school. For more information or to register go to www.collegeboard.com ▶ Many colleges offer options to obtain college credit for life experience. A portfolio of your learning experiences is one possible option.
❐ **Grants and Loans** ➜ Are you wondering how you would pay for college? ➜ Are you interested in finding out more about government funding that is specifically designed to help persons who would normally not be able to afford college go to school?	▶ Pell Grants: This is a federal grant good for private and public college undergraduate studies or for vocational schools approved by the United States Department of Education. **The school must be accredited for you to qualify. This money does not need to be paid back.** The money can be used for tuition, books, or living expenses. The amount awarded depends on your financial need based upon your previous year's earnings. Up to $4,050 (July 1, 2004, to June 30, 2005) may be awarded per year. For more information on financial aid go to: http://studentaid.ed.gov To apply on-line for the Pell Grant go to: FAFSA (Free Application For Student Aid): http://www.fafsa.ed.gov/ or phone the Federal Student Aid Information Center at: **1-800-4-FED-AID (1-800-433-3243).** If you are hearing-impaired and have questions please contact the TTY line at **1-800-730-8913.** If you need extra help, contact the school's financial aid department.

Challenges	Help with Challenges
EDUCATION ❏ **Grants and Loans:** www.ed.gov → Do you need help paying for tuition? → Would you be interested in low interest loans which you do not need to pay back immediately?	▶ Stafford Loans: Subsidized and Unsubsidized. These loans are available for undergraduate and graduate students. You do not start repayment until six months after you finish school. ▶ Subsidized Subsidized loans are need-based. The federal government pays the interest on these loans while the student is in school and during the grace period before repayment begins. ▶ Unsubsidized For students who don't qualify for subsidized loans. The borrower is responsible for interest on such a loan as soon as it is taken out. Most of the terms and conditions of subsidized and unsubsidized Stafford loans are the same. Many banks offer these loans. Go to **www.salliemae.com** and **www.chasemanhattan.com**
❏ **Internships and Fellowships** → Do you lack work experience to get a job in your field? → Are you still in school or planning to enter a graduate program?	▶ Internships: Internships are an excellent way to obtain work experience and college credit at the same time. Many schools have internship programs in a variety of occupational fields including medical, research, international studies, technical, technology, languages, social services, and other areas. You can search for internships and fellowships on the Internet. Some internships are subsidized, meaning that you may receive a salary or assistance with room and board while working. Fellowships are usually for more advanced studies for students in Masters and Ph.D. programs. programs.

> ***On this page, list your personal challenges, then list the help available to you.*** *Make a commitment to seek help and to begin dealing with and overcoming those challenges.*

List Your Personal Challenges	Help With Your Personal Challenges
☐	☐
☐	☐
☐	☐
☐	☐

HIDDEN CHALLENGES

Not all vocational challenges are visible. The nice thing about having a hidden disability is that you will not be directly discriminated against because of your disability. The bad part is that you may not realize that you have a disability.

People with hidden disabilities often feel as if they are misunderstood or different. You may be wondering why you are having difficulty working in certain types of environments or performing certain tasks. You may have had difficulty maintaining employment.

Once you understand your challenges, it will become easier for you to identify jobs that are right for you, and you will be better able to manage your condition in the workplace.

Do You Have a Psychiatric Disability?

Individuals with psychiatric disabilities have varying challenges depending on the severity of their condition, degree of family and community support, medication, and awareness and acceptance of their condition.

Common Psychiatric Disabilities	Workplace Strengths
OCD: Obsessive-Compulsive Disorder. People with OCD are troubled by obsessive, repetitive thoughts and compulsive actions, such as cleaning, checking, counting, or hoarding	Excels in jobs that are very detail-oriented and require high accuracy, such as accounting and medical records.
AUTISM: People who have difficulty communicating with others due to an inability to understand social cues. Loss of sensory perception of extremities.	Works best in jobs that require minimum social interaction, working with animals, truck driving, research, data management, or computer programming. May excel in music.
BI-POLAR/ MANIC-DEPRESSIVE: People who go from extreme depression to extreme high energy—dramatic mood swings.	People who remain untreated work best in jobs that require, at times, a high level of energy and flexible work hours. Individuals who have bi-polar disorder are often very creative. Bi-polar persons who are stabilized on their medications can work in any profession.
SCHIZOPHRENIA/PARANOIA: Persons with these conditions have trust issues and should not be pushed.	Persons with these conditions work best in jobs where there is little conflict and where they work with a small team. These workers may exhibit exceptional concentration and drive.

Do You Have a Learning Disability?

What is a learning disability?

The term *learning disabled* applies to a wide variety of disabling conditions that impact a person's ability to learn.

Does this mean that people with learning disabilities cannot learn?

No. It means that people with a learning disability will learn better if the work environment and training is adjusted to accommodate their *particular learning style.*

What do you mean by "learning style"?

Some people learn best by reading, others remember better through hearing, and some people learn best by doing or from hands-on instruction. *All people have preferred learning styles.*

What should I tell my employer?

It may not be necessary to disclose your learning disability unless your particular accommodation needs are above and beyond what an employer would normally provide in training new workers or when teaching a specific task.

Many larger employers already use a variety of teaching styles when training staff. Smaller employers often rely on only one style of instruction, which may not be the best way for everyone to learn.

> If you know how you learn best—be proactive!
> If a company teaches orally and you learn visually, ask for written materials or take lots of notes. Another option is to ask if you can record the instructions to playback later.

> The disability you do not want to face
> may be exactly what is
> keeping you from getting and retaining
> the job you really want.

If you are having trouble managing your emotions:

► Consider mental health counseling to learn coping strategies and to help you work through your particular issues.

► Would you be better off working with data or things rather than people?

► Are there any new medical treatments for your disability?

► Regular exercise can help you reduce feelings of depression and anxiety.

If you are having trouble being part of the team:

► Tell your co-workers and supervisors that you are shy and sometimes feel uncomfortable at first.

► Ask for a mentor: *"Is there a specific staff person that I could go to if I have questions about my work tasks?"*

► Practice making small talk with your co-workers. For example:
   Did you have a nice weekend?
   What are you doing this weekend?
   What are you having for lunch?
   Do you want me to pick up lunch for you?

Common Learning Disabilities	Common Workplace Issues
ADHD: Attention deficit disorder with Hyperactivity	Problems working in stationary Positions
ADD: Attention deficit disorder	Difficulty staying on task, concentrating on a specific task, organizing work area and home
DYSLEXIA: May see letters or numbers backward or off the page	Reading, spelling, mathematics
AUDITORIAL/ PERCEPTUAL: Affects ability to interpret and process information through the sense of hearing	Problems with verbal instructions: people with this type of disability often hear inaccurately. For example, if you say, *"I starred in the Nutcracker,"* the person might hear, *"I started in the Nutcracker."*

Consider These Accommodations	Strengths
ADHD: Checklists Varying job duties	Higher creativity High intellectual ability Good sense of humor
ADD: Quiet work area with few distractions (such as foot traffic and conversation) Jobs that involve physical activity Flexibility in work tasks	Ability to focus for long periods of time in areas of interest Heightened ability for problem-solving and reasoning
DYSLEXIA: Verbal instructions Using spell check on the computer	May have above average motor coordination, spatial ability or sense of hearing
AUDITORIAL/ PERCEPTUAL: Written instructions, repetition	May have excellent visual memory

Now that you know that you may have a hidden disability, you can start changing the way you handle it.

> ## Focus on solutions that will help you function better.

If you have trouble sitting still:

▶ Can you take an exercise break instead of a coffee break?

▶ Can you vary your work duties to accommodate your restlessness?

▶ Will medication help?

▶ Would a more physical job be more suitable for you?

▶ If your disability affects your ability to work in a busy environment, asking for a quieter work space or changing the position of your desk could spell the difference between your success and failure on the job.

If you are having trouble hearing accurately, these strategies may help:

▶ *"I am not sure I understood you correctly, would you mind repeating?"*

▶ Rephrase in your own words what you heard. *"Is this what you mean?"*

▶ Ask for written instructions. *"I remember things better when they are written down. Do you have any written instructions?"*

▶ *"Would you mind putting this in an e-mail to me?"*

If learning new tasks is difficult:

▶ *"It takes me a little longer at first to learn something new. Is there something I could work on at home while I am learning?"*

▶ *"I learn best when I learn one thing at a time. Would you mind slowing down just a little?"*

Humans are not all made alike. Each person has his or her own special qualities.

One person may be very athletic and have strong legs and arms, but have a slow mind.

Another person might be creative and have a quick mind, but have no feet to stand on.

The nice thing about being a unique individual is that different jobs require different abilities.

CAN TECHNOLOGY HELP?

Many people with disabilities have been helped by advances in technology. For example, people with writing and spelling difficulties no longer have to embarrass themselves with poorly written letters and notes. The use of spell check makes it easier to accommodate yourself.

Did you know that there are many other technological advances which will help you accommodate your particular challenges?

Can Technology Help You?

Help for persons with back pain, neck pain, and shoulder pain:

Ergonomic chairs: Many types of ergonomic chairs make sitting less painful for persons with physical challenges.

Gel cushions: Seats are made of gel material.

Headrests and armrests: Some chairs have headrests that support the upper back, neck, or arms.

Alternative-shaped chairs: One chair that many people find comfortable has a cut-out in the back of the chair which alleviates pressure on the back.

Height adjustable desks: By changing the height of the desk, a person's posture while working can be improved. Desk heights can be changed by putting a platform under the desk or chair, trimming the legs on the desk or by using a customized fabrication.

Help for persons with neck problems:

Headsets: Headsets used to be rare in the workplace, but now most major call centers in the United States use them as a mandatory piece of equipment. Instead of having to tilt your head to talk and type, a headset allows a person to maintain a natural posture while talking on the phone. Once you use one, you will never want to work without it. Headsets are available at all electronics and office supply stores.

Technology has helped many physically challenged individuals and individuals with learning disabilities to become much more independent and functional.

Help for persons with carpal tunnel or other handling difficulties:

Touch Screens
Devices placed on the computer monitor (or built into it) that allow a person to get around on the computer by touching the screen.

Alternative Keyboards
- Larger or smaller than standard keys
- Variously shaped keyboards
- Alternative key configurations
- Keyboards for use with one hand

Trackballs
Moveable balls on top of a base that can be used to move the cursor on the screen.

Joysticks
Different types of joysticks allow you to control the cursor on the screen using hand, feet, or chin.

Help for persons with spelling, reading and language difficulties:

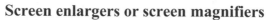

Talking and large-print word processors
Software programs that present graphics and text as speech. A screen reader is used to verbalize or "speak," everything on the screen including names and descriptions of control buttons, menus, text, and punctuation.

Screen enlargers or screen magnifiers
These work like a magnifying glass. They enlarge a portion of the screen as the user moves the pointer, increasing legibility for some users. Some screen enlargers allow a user to zoom in and out on a particular area of the monitor screen.

Help for persons with spelling, reading and language difficulties.

franklin.com

Electronic Dictionaries
Can be found at most office supply stores. These dictionaries are portable and can be carried with you in your purse or pocket.

Phonetic Spell Correction
This feature allows users to type in a word the way it sounds and receive a correction list. For example, *nolij* will find "knowledge"; *kaufee* will find "coffee," and so on.

Speaking Spelling and Handwriting Ace™
Pronounces and correctly spells 80,000 words for auditory reinforcement. Keyboard echo lets you hear each letter pronounced as the key is pressed. Rhyme-key lists words that rhyme with the entered word.

Wizcomtech.com

The Reading Pen
Lightweight and can be held in your hand. It will scan a word, read it aloud, spell it aloud, display it by syllables and display and speak the dictionary definition. Guided by an easy-to-read menu, the user can control the volume, pitch and speed at which the word will be read aloud.

Speech Recognition Systems
Also called Voice Recognition programs, they allow users to give commands and enter data using their voices rather than a mouse or keyboard.

Don't forget to spell/grammar check!

Can Technology Help?

Knox Learning Center
SW Tech Library Services67
1800 Bronson Boulevard
Fennimore, WI 53809

Smartphones

Smartphones have opened up communication options for everyone. Its unique ability to identify the users' exact location and answer questions about their environment greatly enhances the quality of daily life for persons who have difficulty seeing, hearing, reading, touching, remembering, or navigating. The intuitiveness of these devices makes them easy to use which is especially helpful for persons with disabilities.

Persons with low vision or other reading difficulties can download apps that read everything to them. Users can get information or send information from their smart phones without having to do anything except talk to their smart phone. Once the smart phone has been set up to accommodate your learning style and communication preferences, your phone will automatically respond to your voice or touch.

By incorporating the use of an interactive keyboard and pictures, persons who have lost the ability to speak can communicate by touch just as easily as a person who communicates by voice. Persons who understand best through kinesthetic learning or learning by doing, can do all sort of things through apps set up to communicate with the user kinesthetically and interactively.

Smart phones make communicating easy for people with all sorts of challenges. For the first time in history, people with challenges can communicate comfortably and efficiently with the same ease as persons without a disability.

Stand up to your obstacles and do something about them. You will find that they haven't half the strength you think they have.

—Norman Vincent Peale

CAREER TRANSITIONS

> Most people have limited knowledge of their employment options other than the jobs that they themselves or their family members have held.
>
> The fact is that there are many different kinds of work out there. By focusing on your skills and abilities, and not just on your job title, you will begin to identify other job goals that build upon your experience, interests, and strengths.
>
> Identifying the right job goal is the key to finding appropriate and satisfying employment.

Transitioning Graduates From School to Work

Fortune 500 Companies

New graduates are still recruited by a number of Fortune 500 businesses. Many businesses have programs designed specifically for graduating students.

For a list of major companies that you can search by city, occupation, or industry, check out **www.hoovers.com**.

Staffing Services and Employment Agencies

Did you know that the second-largest employer in the United States is a staffing service?

Many companies use employment agencies for their recruiting. In the past, many employers hired "temps" to fill a position temporarily, that is, to fill in for an absent employee. The length of the job varied from one day to a few weeks.

Although staffing companies still fill temporary positions, many employment agencies now are filling what are called "temp-to-perm" positions. Usually a person will work about three months as an employee paid through the staffing service. After the three-month probation period, the person may become a company employee.

The major advantage for employers is that they have a chance to try you out before hiring you, without the expense and time required to screen applicants, interview people, complete paperwork, and file tax and payroll information.

The advantage for you, as a new graduate, is that you can try working in a business without having to commit to working there on a permanent basis. You have the opportunity as a temp to be exposed to a variety of work environments. It works both ways. Getting some diversified work experience will help you find just where and how you best fit into the workplace.

What if the work I find is not in my major?

Although some people find jobs in their major, graduates often end up working in jobs that are unrelated to their majors.

Higher education does not always pay off immediately in the job market, but a degree is still more than just a piece of paper. Here is what a degree reveals. It says you have the ability to:

- ❏ Work with deadlines
- ❏ Manage multiple priorities
- ❏ Work independently
- ❏ Research information
- ❏ Understand new concepts
- ❏ Analyze information
- ❏ Study skills
- ❏ Follow assignments

- ❏ Organize work
- ❏ Follow through from start to finish
- ❏ Read complex matter
- ❏ Use advanced mathematics
- ❏ Memorize information
- ❏ Effectively carry out written and verbal communication
- ❏ _____
- ❏ _____

Remember, even if your education is not immediately recognized in the workplace, it does not take away the value of what you have learned.
You can lose a job, your house, or even a loved one, but nothing can take away what you have learned.

Transitioning From an Advanced Degree

Advanced Degree

As there are only so many job postings where an employer is specifically looking for a person with a Ph.D., M.B.A., or J.D., it may be necessary to look for jobs that are not directly related to your field of study.

Keep an open mind.

People with advanced degrees can find jobs in business, government, education, private agencies, and just about anywhere people need someone with an advanced ability to reason, study, analyze, and research.

If your credentials are higher than or different from what a job description demands, they may "overwhelm" a prospective employer. It is not mandatory to list all of your credentials; you may list only those which are required for a particular position.

You can also list your education near the bottom of your resume to draw more attention to your qualifications and work history.

For example:

Jenny Milton has just passed the bar exam and she is now licensed to practice law in Ohio. Unfortunately, the job market there is weak for attorneys, and she does not want to move.

In evaluating some of her qualifications, it was noted that she has advanced skills in reading and researching complex material, negotiation, interviewing, and analysis. Her written and verbal communication skills are top-notch.

These same skills would be helpful in positions including human resources, mediation, procurement, grant writing, provider contracting with an HMO or PPO, or legal software sales.

Be creative. Your skills are valuable to the right employer.

Transitioning From a Highly Specialized Field

> The higher your previous salary and/or education, the lower will be the number of suitable jobs will be available for you in the local labor market.

Highly Specialized

For example:

Barry Felman, a CEO of a large hospital, loses his job due to a merger. Unfortunately, there is only one other hospital in the town. They are not looking to add any executive level positions, nor would Barry want to work there.

Barry will either have to move or diversify into other management arenas, perhaps in a nursing home, medical equipment firm, or medical non-profit.

Is moving an option for you?

A geographical move may be the only way to find a job that is a perfect fit. With a global market, people with highly specialized skills are needed in all parts of the world.

If moving is not an option, a career change may be in order.

Whether you expand your current specialty, find a job in a previous occupation, or return to school to learn something new, expect to spend a month of job searching for every $10,000 in annual salary expectations.

Transitioning from Military to Civilian Jobs

Life in the military

Because military personnel may encounter very dangerous conditions in the course of their work, it is essential that all military personnel strictly adhere to rules and regulations.

Disobeying or questioning authority in the military is not permissible and is even punishable by military laws.

To be successful in battle, troops must work together and present a united front to overcome the enemy. Since you may need to respond quickly to avoid danger, regimentation and teamwork may save your life.

If fellow soldiers make a mistake when they are doing their job in the military, you may find yourself in a very dangerous situation. It is important not only for you to be accurate and precise, but also for your fellow troops to be accurate and precise.

In the military, being precise and regimented is essential.

Adjusting to civilian life

In civilian jobs, being precise and regimented is not usually as important as in military life. Although there are some jobs where a life may be at stake if you are inattentive or stray from the rules, usually the consequences of an individual's actions are much less severe.

Most jobs in the civilian world require more flexibility than is permissible in the military.

In civilian work, going with the flow, and changing or adapting rules and practices according to the situation is often more important than being precise. Trying to make sure that your co-workers are doing things perfectly can create tension and conflict with co-workers.

Learning to use social skills will help you advance in your civilian career. In a global market, your knowledge of other cultures and your ability to adjust is especially important. Try incorporating your knowledge, and be open to learning new skills.

In the civilian world, questioning how things are done and finding new ways of doing things may actually help your employers by giving them the cutting edge in business.

Military Job Titles

Intelligence

General Officer

Recon Specialist

Tankers, Bombers

Training Commander

Communications

Warrant Officer

Security Forces

Contracting

Snipers

Translating those skills and abilities you used while in the military into civilian language

Provided security

Operated heavy equipment

Investigated security risks

Analyzed information

Team-worker

Physically fit

Transitioning from military to civilian jobs

Maintained equipment

Exceptional hand-eye coordination

Purchased supplies for military base

Supervised team leaders

Strategizing company goals

Recruited new personnel

Trained team members

Civilian Job Titles

Driver

Engineer

Recruiter

Management

Security Guard

Public Relations

Technical Manager

Warehouse Worker

Heavy Equipment Operator

Technical Specialist

Purchasing

Detective

Trainer

Police

FBI

Transitioning From Stay-at-Home Parent or Caregiver Back Into the Workplace

Many people choose or need to leave the workforce to raise children or care for elderly parents. Often the first barrier to returning to paid employment is identifying and acknowledging what you did while caring for your loved ones. *Check the responsibilities that apply and describe your job:*

❐ Did you coordinate schedules and appointments for multiple family members?

❐ Did you pay bills?

❐ Did you manage a budget and implement cost savings through analyzing purchasing options?

❐ Did you researched community resources and now know a great deal about social services?

❐ Did you gain specialized knowledge about a mental, physical, or emotional condition during this time?

❐ Did you prepared special diets because a loved one had diabetes, high cholesterol, swallowing difficulties, or allergies?

❐ Did you learn about Medicare and Medicaid guidelines?

❐ Are you patient, dependable and reliable?

You may also have gained valuable experience while volunteering for your children's PTA or Cub Scout troop.

❒ Were you involved in a fund-raising drive?

❒ Did you recruit and coordinate volunteers?

❒ Did you organize and plan a trip for over 50 people?

❒ Did you lead group activities?

❒ Did you head or participate in a committee?

❒ Did you oversee the phone tree?

❒ Did you run a program at your child's school?

❒ Did you help in your child's classroom?

Even though you were not paid for the hours you worked, it does *not* mean the experience, knowledge, and skills you developed are not valuable in the workplace. They may be the exact skills and abilities an employer needs.

Transitioning From Lay-Off

Many people want to find careers because their industries have died out due to technology or a lack of demand or because their jobs have gone overseas.

Just because your industry or profession has disappeared, it does not mean that you do not have sought-after skills. For example:

If you were a manager of a manufacturing plant, your duties probably included these types of responsibilities:

▶ Managing personnel, including department heads and supervisors

▶ Prioritizing work: arranging the work-flow according to time schedules and deadlines

▶ Ensuring the quality of work meets customer specifications

▶ Calculating work hours and materials to maintain and increase profitability

▶ Understanding and using advanced technologies to ensure competitiveness in industry

Compare this to the duties of the manager of a business office:

▶ Managing personnel, including department heads and supervisors

▶ Prioritizing work: arranging the work-flow according to time schedules and deadlines

▶ Ensuring the quality of work meets customer specifications

▶ Calculating work hours and materials to maintain and increase profitability

▶ Understanding and using advanced technologies to ensure competitiveness in industry

As you can see, the primary functions of the jobs are identical.

While your specific industry or product background may not transition to your next employer, *your knowledge* of manufacturing processes and procedures may be completely transferable.

Even if your background is not a precise match, your experience as a manager may be quite valuable to your next employer.

Transferable skills do not only apply to managerial positions. Perhaps you were an electronic assembler in the manufacturing plant. Your transferable skills probably included something like this:

▶ Microscopic assembling according to precision industry standards

▶ Able to maintain quotas in a fast-paced production environment

▶ Reading diagrams and assembling according to blueprint specifications

▶ Perform work requiring a high level of hand-eye coordination

Compare this to the duties of an assembler of medical products, such as pacemakers or heart valves:

▶ Microscopic assembling according to precision industry standards

▶ Able to maintain quotas in a fast-paced production environment

▶ Reading diagrams and assembling according to blueprint specifications

▶ Perform work requiring a high level of hand-eye coordination

Slow Learners

Not all jobs require a high level of functioning. Some people are born with diseases such as Down Syndrome and other people may have deficits due to a head injury or a disease.*

Jobs that best suit persons with these types of challenges are positions that require the completion of simple, routine tasks.

Listed below are some jobs that require little decision-making, reasoning or problem-solving.

Dishwasher	Stocker
Yard crew	Kennel worker
Janitorial	Cafeteria server
Housekeeping	Ticket taker
Assembly	Bindery
Sorter	Bagger
Farm helper	Construction helper

A good job fit gives people a sense of purpose,
allows people to be self-supporting and provides an
opportunity to interact in a meaningful way with other adults
and the community.

*As people have varying degrees of intellectual abilities, it is helpful to obtain a thorough understanding of a person's abilities through standardized testing and work sampling. Some people may be able to work only in a sheltered work environment with trained supervisors, while others may be able to work in competitive employment.

Transitioning Into a Low-stress Job

Low-stress jobs

If you are experiencing emotional issues such as severe anxiety, depression, post-traumatic stress disorder, recovery from alcohol, drugs, or burnout, it may be better for you to work in a less stressful job until you have some recovery behind you.

People who have been unemployed for more than six months may find that their job search is very stressful. Most people get discouraged and experience a great deal of stress during long periods of unemployment. Sometimes part-time work in a job that is not too demanding will give you the boost you need to maintain emotional balance during a prolonged job search until you get the job you really want.

What do you mean by a "low-stress" job?

Stress is different for each individual. While one person might find working in a fast-paced job stressful, other people thrive in a fast-paced position.

Jobs that involve a lot of responsibility, decision-making, problem-solving, risk taking, and deadlines are considered stressful by most people.

I like what I do, but I find it stressful where I currently work.

Sometimes stress is relative to a particular employer. Sources of stress may include personnel shortages, insufficient funding, long work hours, poor staff training, too much responsibility for too little pay, or poor management.

Transitioning From Heavy Work to Sedentary/Light Work

The inability to do heavy work may be keeping you from working in your previous career. You may have been injured in battle, work, or perhaps you simply want to be in a less physical job as you get older. The following jobs might be suitable for you if you have lifting restrictions.

Circle those occupations that interest you or which may be appropriate:

Manufacturing

Assembly

Soldering

Microscopic assembly

Quality control

Engineer

Tool design

Clerical

Word processor

Data entry

Secretary

Bookkeeper

Receptionist

Customer service

Sales and Management

Sales representative

Sales clerk

Marketing

Real estate agent

Insurance agent

Business manager

Consultant

Financial planner

Designer

Hospitality

Host

Cashier

Hotel manager

Events coordinator

Front desk

Reservationist

Travel agent

Technology

Computer programmer

Technical support

Electronic repair

Robotics

Purchasing

Artistic

Actor

Writer

Graphic artist

Musician

Agent

Artist

Jeweler

Knowing your physical limitations, circle those occupations that interest you or which may be appropriate:

Professional
- Rehabilitation counselor
- Attorney
- Teacher
- Minister
- Social worker
- Accountant
- Architect
- Scientist
- Human resources

Medical
- Admissions
- Quality assurance
- Respiratory therapist
- Ward clerk
- Medical lab tech
- Dental lab tech
- Dietician
- Speech pathologist
- Ultrasound tech
- Home health or sitter
- Patient care coordinator
- Audiologist

Paraprofessional
- Paralegal
- Teacher's aide
- Drafting
- Environmental technician

Miscellaneous
- Mortgage clerk
- Title clerk
- Loan officer
- Telemarketer
- Seamstress
- Motorcycle mechanic
- Boat mechanic
- Electric tool repair
- Driver
- Inspector
- Purchasing
- Locksmith
- Security officer
- Construction superintendent
- Insurance adjuster
- Neon tube bender
- Cosmetologist

No one job will fit all persons. Although persons with disabilities may have somewhat different needs, people in certain types of jobs tend to have similar interests and skill sets. These job matches may be appropriate for an individual with lifting restrictions.

Previous Job	Possible Career	Where to Find Job	Retraining
Truck Driver	Courtesy driver	Automobile dealerships	No
		Laser surgery centers	No
	Medicaid drivers	Taxi companies	No
	Chauffeur	Limousine companies	No
	Shuttling cars	Automobile rental companies	No
	Delivery	Automobile parts	No
		Pizza	No
		Dental labs	No
	Tractor-trailer	Companies that specialize in hook & drop delivery	Maybe
	Dump truck driver	Construction companies	OJT*
	Cement truck drivers	Paving companies	OJT
	Recycling truck driver	Recycling companies	OJT
Carpenter	Cabinet Laminating	Cabinet shops	OJT
	Frame making	Art and frame shops	OJT
	Building inspector	City government	May require
		HUD	licensing
	AutoCad drafting	Engineering firms	Yes
Drywall	AutoCad drafting	Engineering and drafting co.	Yes
	Painting	Construction/painting co.	OJT
Autobody Technician	Dental lab technician	Dental labs	OJT
	Pinstriping	Custom shops	No
Cook	Web Site Design	Major employers	Yes
Welder	Soldering	Assembly companies	Yes or OJT
	Dental lab technician	Dental labs	OJT
	Locksmith	Locksmith companies	OJT

*OJT = On-the-job training

Actual physical requirements will vary according to the individual employer
and custom accommodations may be necessary.

Previous Job	Possible Career	Where to Find Job	Retraining
Mechanic	Repair dialysis machines	Dialysis companies	OJT
	Electric tool repair	Tool repair shops	OJT
	Computer repair	Computer stores	Possible OJT
		Major employers	or Retraining
	Small engine repair	Marine dealers	Retraining
		Lawn mower shops	
		Country clubs	
		City government	
Nurse	Quality Assurance	Insurance companies	May need
	Case manager	Rehabilitation companies	computer skills
		Hospitals	
		Government clinics	May need state
		Hospitals	licensing
		Government clinics	
		Schools	
		Physical therapy centers	
		Physician's offices	
Plumber	Inside sales	Plumbing supply co.	Computer skills
	Dispatcher	Plumbing companies	May need
			computer skills
	Estimator	Construction/plumbing	

Possible job matches for an individual with handling or typing restrictions.

Typist	Receptionist	Businesses	No
		Auto dealership	No
	Leasing agent	Apartment complexes	No
	Customer service	Retail	OJT
		Call centers	Maybe
	Front desk	Hotels	OJT
		Fitness center	No
	Spa attendant	Resorts and hotels	No
	Child care worker	Day care centers	May need state or
	Companion	Home health agencies	local licensing

Summing Up Your Job Skills

In summing up your skills, both you and your prospective employer will know exactly what you can and cannot do. In fact, many staffing services use similar forms to assess your skills. *Check all the skills below that apply to you:*

Computer Skills

What software do you use?

- ❏ Word
- ❏ Word Perfect
- ❏ Windows
- ❏ Excel
- ❏ Power Point
- ❏ Adobe Photoshop
- ❏ PageMaker
- ❏ Outlook Express or other web mail program
- ❏ QuickBooks
- ❏ Computerized Inventory
- ❏ Internet Explorer and other browsers or search engines
- ❏ Access or other database programs
- ❏ Oracle
- ❏ Java
- ❏ ADP
- ❏ PeopleSoft
- ❏ AutoCAD
- ❏ _____

Office Skills

- ❏ Typing speed _____wpm
- ❏ Do you do data entry
- ❏ How many keystrokes per hour?_____
- ❏ Can you do ten-key by touch?

Office Equipment

- ❏ Fax
- ❏ Copier
- ❏ Calculator

Money and Financial Skills

- ❏ Cash handling
- ❏ Operated a cash register
- ❏ Credit card processing
- ❏ Balanced daily ledgers or cash registers
- ❏ Processed payments over the phone or Internet
- ❏ Prepared a budget
- ❏ Managed a budget
- ❏ Prepared payroll
- ❏ Bill-paying
- ❏ Managed profit/loss
- ❏ Estimated labor costs
- ❏ Calculated material costs
- ❏ Increased business revenues

Building/Manufacturing

- ❏ Assembly
- ❏ Installation
- ❏ Read blueprints
- ❏ Measure to specifications
- ❏ Quality Control
- ❏ Operate saws, lathes, grinders, and drills
- ❏ Read meters or gauges
- ❏ Repair defective merchandise or goods

Equipment

- ❏ Can you operate heavy equipment?
- ❏ Bulldozer – To grade?
- ❏ Crane
- ❏ Cherry picker
- ❏ Tractor
- ❏ Forklift
- ❏ Truck
- ❏ Punch presses
- ❏ Machine operator
- ❏ _____

Certifications

- ❏ Forklift
- ❏ ASE mechanics
- ❏ OSHA
- ❏ Notary
- ❏ ISO
- ❏ Soldering
- ❏ Technical
- ❏ Computer certifications
- ❏ Professional
- ❏ _____

Licenses

- ❏ Class A driver's license
- ❏ Class B or passenger endorsement
- ❏ Safe Driver's License
- ❏ Professional
- ❏ Trade
- ❏ Business

Whether these skills were learned on or off the job, employers hire people who can get the job done. *Check all the skills below that apply to you:*

People Skills

- ❑ Accept supervision
- ❑ Collaborated on project
- ❑ Customer service
- ❑ Interviewed employment applicants
- ❑ Trained new employees
- ❑ Team leader/Team builder
- ❑ Team player
- ❑ Counsel individuals
- ❑ Motivate clients or workers
- ❑ Handled irate or dissatisfied customers
- ❑ Negotiate services or conditions
- ❑ Persuade to buy or agree
- ❑ Build relationships
- ❑ Close sales
- ❑ Coordinated staff, volunteers, meetings
- ❑ _____

Time Management Skills

- ❑ Plan events or projects
- ❑ Prioritize work in order of importance
- ❑ Schedule work projects
- ❑ Work independently
- ❑ Multi-tasking
- ❑ Finish assignments or projects on time
- ❑ Punctual
- ❑ Reliable

Communication

- ❑ Take accurate messages
- ❑ Answer multiple phone lines
- ❑ Respond to customer inquires
- ❑ High volume call center
- ❑ Cold calling
- ❑ Write business letters
- ❑ Prepared proposals or reports
- ❑ Ability to interact with persons of diverse backgrounds
- ❑ Chair a meeting or a committee
- ❑ Public speaking
- ❑ Public relations
- ❑ Marketing
- ❑ Fluent in Spanish
- ❑ Fluent in French
- ❑ Fluent in other languages (list)
- ❑ _____

Data Management

- ❑ Track inventory
- ❑ Keep accurate records
- ❑ Work with highly detailed information
- ❑ Maintain confidential Information

Security

- ❑ Maintained workplace safety
- ❑ Served on company safety committee
- ❑ Security clearance
- ❑ Maintained law and order
- ❑ Loss prevention

Leadership

- ❑ Hiring and firing
- ❑ Scheduling
- ❑ Decision-making
- ❑ Managed workers and work flow
- ❑ Organized workers or work flow
- ❑ Identified trends
- ❑ Supervised workers, department heads, others
- ❑ Maintained or obtained licenses or contracts
- ❑ Represented business or agency in community or governmental affairs
- ❑ Visualized business growth and direction
- ❑ Assumed fiscal responsibility

Investigative/Analytical

- ❑ Analyze costs or projects
- ❑ Research information
- ❑ Interpret information
- ❑ Investigate
- ❑ Identify trends
- ❑ Problem-solving
- ❑ Statistical analysis
- ❑ Trouble-shooting

Creativity

- ❑ Conceived new way of providing a service
- ❑ Developed or identified new product
- ❑ Designed program
- ❑ Created material

Look before you leap.

—Aesop

GOING BACK TO SCHOOL

Do you lack the skills and/or education you need to get the job of your dreams?

Let's take a look at whether or not going back to school is a good option for you.

Is Going Back to School a Good Option For You?

Check all the reasons that apply to you.

These are some of the reasons why people go back to school.

You can no longer work in your profession due to a physical or emotional limitation that keeps you from performing the essential functions of the job.	There is a high unemployment rate within your field, trade, or profession.
You are having trouble finding a job that matches your skills and abilities.	When you were young, you never had the opportunity to pursue an education.

Your needs may have changed.

You want to work a different shift.	You want something more stable.	You want a job in a growth field.
You want to earn more money.	You want a job with more challenges.	You just want to do something different.
Your children are grown.	You need better benefits.	You are burnt out.
You are in a dead-end job.	Your employer is going bankrupt or selling the company.	Your work is too stressful.

You can often change careers without going back to school.

Many people think that if they can no longer work in their field, that they will be unable to work at all; or they may think that going back to school is their only option.

Many people are also under the false impression that if they get retrained, then they will automatically have a good job when they graduate.

Before you jump into a training program you should consider:

Going back to school is not a guarantee of employment.	It will be easier if you have some emotional support from your family and friends.
Going back to school takes a lot of time and money.	The best predictor of future job satisfaction is previous job satisfaction.
There is no guarantee that you will really like working in that field.	You will still need to look for a job after you graduate.

You may not need retraining. Have you considered...

Another position with your current employer?	Would any of your previous jobs be suitable for you now?
Other jobs related to your background and work experience?	Going back to work for a former employer?

Getting Into School

Follow these steps for returning to school:

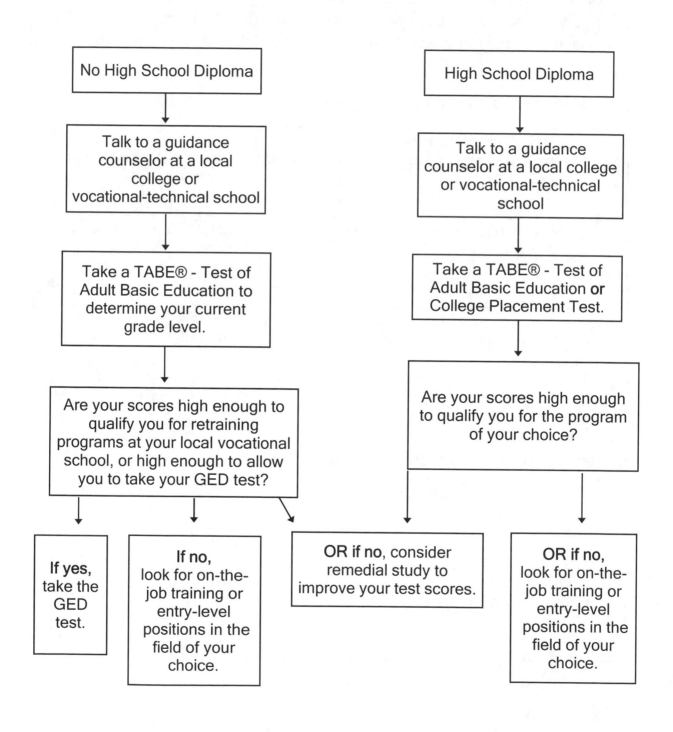

Choosing the Right Training

Take your time before jumping into a program.
First Follow these steps:

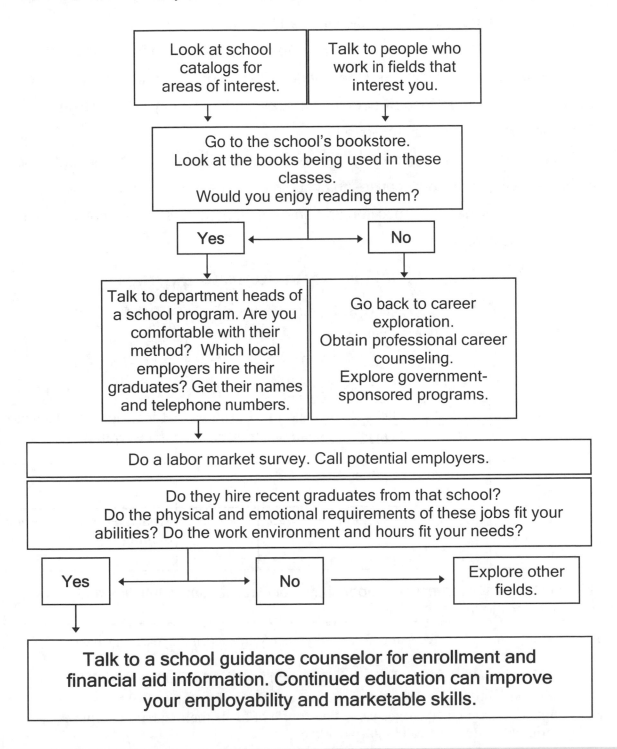

Look at school catalogs for areas of interest.

Talk to people who work in fields that interest you.

Go to the school's bookstore.
Look at the books being used in these classes.
Would you enjoy reading them?

Yes

No

Talk to department heads of a school program. Are you comfortable with their method? Which local employers hire their graduates? Get their names and telephone numbers.

Go back to career exploration.
Obtain professional career counseling.
Explore government-sponsored programs.

Do a labor market survey. Call potential employers.

Do they hire recent graduates from that school?
Do the physical and emotional requirements of these jobs fit your abilities? Do the work environment and hours fit your needs?

Yes

No

Explore other fields.

Talk to a school guidance counselor for enrollment and financial aid information. Continued education can improve your employability and marketable skills.

Fastest Growing Occupations

Below are some government statistics on what fields employ the largest number of people. Use them only as a guide. They may not apply to the area where you live, and even the best statistics and predictions can be wrong.

For example: Computer-related fields were once projected to be the fastest-growing occupational fields in the United States. No one predicted then that many of these positions would be filled by people overseas, and that many highly trained professionals would be left unemployed.

The Internet is changing the way the world does business. With the advent of new technologies, we can expect changes to occur in almost every industry.

Generally, any hands-on position and any work that requires direct contact with people will remain viable career options.

Fastest Growing Occupations Requiring Work Experience or On-the-Job Training*

Listed below are occupations 1-28 of the 323 occupations (requiring work experience or on-the-job training) projected to grow most rapidly during the years 2002-2012.

Go to **www.acinet.org** for more information.

#	Occupation	Employment		Percent change *	Earnings Quartile**	Most significant source of education or training
		2002	**2012**			
1.	Medical assistants	364,600	579,400	59%	—	Moderate-term on-the-job training
2.	Social and human service assistants	305,200	453,900	49%	—	Moderate-term on-the-job training

*Published by the Department of Labor, Office of Occupational Statistics and Employment Projections

**The quartile rankings of Occupational Employment Statistics annual earnings data are presented in the following categories:

$$$$ = Very high ($41,820 and over) $$$ = High ($27,500 to $41,780)

$$ = Low ($19,710 to $27,380) $ = Very low (up to $19,600)

The rankings were based on quartiles using one-fourth of total employment to define each quartile. Earnings are for wage and salary workers.

#	Occupation	Employment		Percent change *	Earnings Quartile**	Most significant source of education or training
		2002	**2012**			
3.	Home health aides	579,700	858,700	48%		Short-term OTJ training
4.	Physical therapist aides	37,000	54,100	46%		Short-term OTJ training
5.	Hazardous materials removal workers	37,600	53,800	43%		Moderate-term OTJ training
6.	Occupational therapist aides	8,300	11,800	43%		Short-term OTJ training
7.	Dental assistants	266,000	379,000	42%	$$	Moderate-term OTJ training
8.	Personal and home care aides	607,6000	853,500	40%	$	Short-term OTJ training
9.	Self-enrichment education teachers	200,400	280,800	40%	$$$	Work experience in a related occupation
10.	Residential advisors	53,100	71,000	34%	$$	Moderate OTJ training
11.	Security guards	995,500	1,312,600	32%	$	Short-term OTJ training
12.	Heating, air conditioning, and refrigeration mechanics and installers	248,700	327,700	32%	$$$	Long-term OTJ training
13.	Receptionists and information clerks	1,100,300	1,424,900	30%	$$	Short-term OTJ training
14.	Pharmacy technicians	210,800	271,500	29%	$$	Work experience in a related occupation
15.	Emergency management	10,900	14,000	28%	$$$$	Work experience in a related occupation

#	Occupation	Employment		Percent change *	Earnings Quartile**	Most significant source of education/training
		2002	2012			
16.	Interviewers, except eligibility and loan	192,900	246,900	28%	$$	Short-term OTJ training
17.	Amusement and recreation attendants	234,000	299,000	28%	$4	Short-term OTJ training
18.	Audio and video equipment technicians	41,800	52,900	27%	$$$	Long-term OTJ training
19.	Ambulance drivers and attendants, except emergency medical technicians	17,100	21,700	27%	$	Moderate-term OTJ training
20.	Locker room, coatroom, and dressing room attendants	23,000	29,000	27%	$	Short-term OTJ training
21.	Tile and marble setters	33,200	42,000	26%	$$$	Short-term OTJ training
22.	Counter and rental clerks	435,800	550,200	26%	$	Short-term OTJ training
23.	Veterinary assistants and laboratory animal caretakers	62,800	79,200	26%	$	Short-term OTJ training
24.	Cement masons and concrete finishers	181,700	229,000	26%	$$$	Moderate-term OTJ training
25.	Private detectives and investigators	48,000	60,200	25%	$$$	Work experience in a related occupation
26.	Costume attendants	3,600	4,500	25%	$$	Short-term OTJ training
27.	Nursing aides, orderlies, attendants	1,375,300	1,718,100	25%	$$	Short-term OTJ training
28.	Police and sheriff's patrol officers	618,800	771,600	25%	$$$	Long-term OTJ training

The fastest growing career fields are further categorized by state and wages. Visit the website www.acinet.org for more detailed information.

Employment Options

| # | Occupation | Employment | | Percent change* | Earnings Quartile** | Most significant source of education or training |
		2002	**2012**			
1.	Medical records and health information technicians	146,900	215,600	47%	$$	Associate degree
2.	Physical therapist assistants	50,200	72,600	45%	$$$	Associate degree
3.	Fitness trainers, aerobics instructors	182,700	263,900	44%	$$	Postsecondary vocational award
4.	Veterinary technologists and technicians	52,700	75,900	44%	$$	Associate degree
5.	Dental hygienists	148,000	211,700	44%	$$	Associate degree
6.	Occupational therapist assistants	18,500	25,700	39%	$$$	Associate degree
7.	Environmental science and protection technicians, including health	27,600	37,700	37%	$$$	Associate degree
8.	Preschool teachers except special ed)	423,600	576,900	36%	$	Postsecondary vocational award
9.	Respiratory therapy technicians	85,800	114,600	35%	$$$	Associate degree
10.	Respiratory therapy technicians	26,400	35,500	34%	$$$	Postsecondary vocational award
11.	Cardiovascular technologists and technicians	43,400	57,900	34%	$$$	Associate degree
12.	Emergency medical techs, paramedics	179,100	238,400	33%	$$	Postsecondary vocational award
13.	Radiation therapists	13,500	17,800	32%	$$$$	Associate degree
14.	Computer support specialists	506,900	660,300	30%	$$$	Associate degree

Fastest-growing Jobs Requiring Post-Secondary Training or an Associate's Degree
Listed below are the top 25 occupations requiring post-secondary education or training below the bachelor's degree projected to grow the fastest during the years 2002-2012.

#	Occupation	Employment		Percent change *	Earnings Quartile**	Most significant source of education or training
		2002	2012			
15.	Security/fire alarm systems installers	46,300	60,300	30%	$$$	Postsecondary vocational award
16.	Desktop publishers	35,000	45,200	29%	$$$	Postsecondary vocational award
17.	Paralegals and legal assistants	199,600	256,900	29%	$$$	Associate Degree
18.	Environmental engineering technicians	19,100	24,500	28%	$$$	Associate Degree
19.	Surgical technologists	72,200	92,400	28%	$$$	Postsecondary vocational award
20.	Registered nurses	2,284,500	2,907600	27%	$$$$	Associate Degree
21.	Massage therapists	92,100	117,000	27%	$$$	Postsecondary vocational award
22.	Sound engineering technicians	12,800	16,200	25%	$$$	Postsecondary vocational award
23.	Gaming dealers	77,900	97,100	25%	$	Postsecondary vocational award
24.	Gaming and sports book writers and runners	14,100	17,500	24%	$	Postsecondary vocational award
25.	Diagnostic medical sonographers	36,500	45,300	24%	$$$$	Associate Degree

**The quartile rankings of Occupational Employment Statistics annual earnings data are presented in the following categories:

$$$$ = Very high ($41,820 and over) $$ = Low ($19,710 to $27,380)

$$$ = High ($27,500 to $41,780) $ = Very low (up to $19,600)

      The rankings were based on quartiles using one-fourth of total employment to define each quartile. The fastest growing career fields are further broken down by state and wages. Visit the website **www.acinet.org** for more detailed information. Earnings are for wage and salary workers.

Fastest-growing Jobs Requiring a Bachelor's Degree or Higher

Listed below are top 25 occupations that generally require bachelor's degree or higher projected to grow the fastest during the years 2002-2012.

#	Occupation	Employment		Percent change *	Earnings Quartile**	Most significant source of education or training
		2002	2012			
1.	Network systems and data communications analysts	186,000	292,000	57%	$$$$	Bachelor's Degree
2.	Physician assistants	63,000	93,800	49%	$$$$	Bachelor's Degree
3.	Computer software engineers, applications	394,100	473,400	46%	$$$$	Bachelor's Degree
4.	Computer software engineers, systems software	281,100	408,900	45%	$$$$	Bachelor's Degree
5.	Database administrators	110,000	158,600	44%	$$$$	Bachelor's Degree
6.	Computer systems analysts	468,300	652,700	39%	$$$$	Bachelor's Degree
7.	Environmental engineers	47,100	65,100	38%	$$$$	Bachelor's Degree
8.	Network and computer systems administrators	251,400	234,300	37%	$$$$	Bachelor's Degree
9.	Computer and information systems managers	284,400	387,000	36%	$$$$	Bachelor's Degree or higher, plus work experience
10.	Physical therapists	136,900	185,200	35%	$$$$	Master's Degree
11.	Occupational therapists	81,600	110,400	35%	$$$$	Bachelor's Degree
12.	Personal financial advisors	126,200	163,500	34%	$$	Bachelor's Degree
13.	Mental health and substance abuse social workers	94,900	127,700	35%	$$$	Master's Degree

#	Occupation	Employment		Percent change *	Earnings Quartile**	Most significant source of education or training
		2002	2012			
14.	Rehabilitation counselors	122,200	163,500	35%	$$	Master's Degree
15.	Survey researchers	20,000	27,100	34%	$$	Master's Degree
16.	Public relations specialists	158,100	210,100	33%	$$$	Bachelor's Degree
17.	Epidemiologists	3,900	5,200	32%	$$$$	Master's Degree
18.	Education administrators, preschool and childcare center/program	58,000	76,500	32%	$$$	Bachelor's Degree or higher, plus work experience
19.	Sales managers	343,000	447,600	30%	$$$$	Bachelor's Degree or higher, plus work experience
20.	Management analysts	577,400	753,100	30%	$$$$	Bachelor's Degree or higher, plus work experience
21.	Pharmacists	230,000	299,400	30%	$$$$	First professional degree
22.	Computer and information scientists, research	23,200	30,200	30%	$$$$	Doctoral Degree
23.	Athletic trainers	14,300	18,500	30%	$$$	Bachelor's Degree
24.	Medical and health services managers	243,600	314,900	29%	$$$$	Bachelor's Degree or higher, plus work experience
25.	Audiologists	10,900	14,100	29%	$$$$	Master's Degree

Be sure to check your labor market, especially in computer-related fields:

Although it is important to consider occupational growth statistics, you should never pick a field based solely on projected employment statistics. Often the most recent projections are already several years old.

What School Should You Choose?

Many types of educational and training programs are available to choose from:

- ❏ Technical School
- ❏ Technical Certification
- ❏ Trade Certification
- ❏ Professional Licensing Program
- ❏ Two-year degree
- ❏ Four-year degree
- ❏ Professional certification program
- ❏ Master's program
- ❏ Ph.D. program

Different schools offer similar programs. Thoroughly check all your local schools to find the best program for you.

You may want to consider some of these short-term programs. Many of them require school attendance for only a few days or weeks. Most of these programs do not have entry requirements, but you may need to pass a test to obtain the licensing or certification.

❏ Class A driver's license	❏ Certified nursing assistant
❏ Mortgage broker's license	❏ Stockbroker's license
❏ Real estate license	❏ Cosmetology license
❏ Security guard license	❏ Massage therapy certification
❏ Insurance agent's license	❏ Stockbroker's license
❏ Insurance adjuster's license	❏ Fitness trainers

Public versus Private School

Should you go to a public school?

REASONS TO ATTEND A PUBLIC SCHOOL

Less expensive
May have more programs to choose from
Credits are usually transferable to another school
It is easier to change majors
More financial aid may be available
More job fairs may be held for new graduates
More internships may be available

REASONS NOT TO ATTEND A PUBLIC SCHOOL

Enrollment can be quite confusing
Parking may be a problem
It might be hard to get information about the different programs
offered
Attention is less personalized (you may feel like a number)

Should you go to a private school?

REASONS TO ATTEND A PRIVATE SCHOOL

Easier to enroll
Programs may be completed in a shorter time
The location may be more convenient
Entry dates may be more frequent and flexible
Smaller programs
Larger staff and more personalized attention
It may be easier to find out about the various programs that the school
offers

REASONS NOT TO ATTEND A PRIVATE SCHOOL

May be more expensive
Job placement assistance may be overrated

☞**USE CAUTION!** Some private schools are **not accredited**. Be sure to ask about accreditation. If you want to continue your education or transfer to another college, you might not be able to transfer your credits.

Can You Find a Job in the Field of Your Choice?

Going back to school is not a guarantee of employment. You may have a friend who went back to school to become a computer programmer. He started in his new career at a high salary. You want to do the same thing.

☞USE CAUTION!! What was a hot labor market a year ago may now be a field where it is almost impossible to get a job.

> You should strongly consider getting <u>five</u> positive responses from potential employers before starting any retraining program.

"But I talked with the school guidance counselor who said that I should enter this program."

School guidance counselors often can be quite helpful at helping students make career choices based upon their interests, backgrounds, and results of standardized tests.

> A school guidance counselor does not always have up-to-date labor market information.

It is also possible that the school you would like to attend may not offer the program that would be the best match for you.

It may be worthwhile to talk to a guidance counselor at several different schools to find the career that is just right for you.

The best way to determine if a retraining option will help you get the job you want is to *call those employers* who would typically hire you after you have finished the program.

Example: Let's say you want to go to school for web design, and you want to work near where you currently live.

▶ Look up **web design** in your city's Yellow Pages.

▶ Call ten companies for whom you would like to work.

▶ Ask to talk directly with the Department Manager you would like to work for or with the Human Resources Department.

Ask questions:

"May I speak to the manager of the IT department?"

"I am considering going to school at _____ for web design training. Have you ever hired anyone out of their program?"

If yes:

▶ *Did you feel that the students were well-trained?*

▶ *Have you hired in the last six months, or do you intend to hire?*

▶ *What is the typical salary range for a new graduate?*

If no:

▶ *Would you consider hiring someone from this program?*

▶ *Have you hired in the last six months, or do you intend to hire?*

▶ *What is the typical salary range for a new graduate?*

Address any vocational obstacles or concerns that you may have, such as:

► *Is this a job where you typically sit or do you typically stand?*

► *Is there a great deal of physical labor involved in this job?*

► *Would you consider hiring someone with an old felony charge?*

► *What is the typical salary range for this position?*

> **If you do not know whom to call, ask the school's program director or your instructor, "*Which employers in the community typically hires your graduates?*"**

Example: You want to go to school to be an electronics technician. Ask the potential employer these questions:

► *I am considering going to school for electronics tech. The program instructor, (use name of instructor), told me that you have hired his students in the past. Is that accurate?*

► *Were you happy with the students you hired?*

► *Are you planning on doing any future hiring in this field?*

If you do not get the positive answers that you expect, consider yourself lucky. You found out <u>before</u> you invested a lot of time or money.

If you have trouble getting information, consider hiring a trained professional to ensure that you are heading in the right direction. Most private vocational evaluators are well-trained in labor market surveys. **Go to www.rehabpro.org** to find a vocational evaluator in your area.

Conduct a Web Search of Jobs That Interest You

The Internet is a tremendously helpful resource for job hunters. Many private and public companies post their job openings and job descriptions on their websites. Local, state and federal governments — by public law — must list the salary ranges of their jobs.

Job descriptions often provide information on minimum educational requirements, salary schedules, as well as the physical and emotional requirements of the job.

These official government websites may help:

www.usajobs.opm.gov — Government job information

www.studentjobs.gov — Student jobs within the federal government

www.doleta.gov — Department of Labor, employment and training information

It is also helpful to check your city, county, and state job listings, which can be found through your search engines like Google and Yahoo.

Other websites for job searches, career information, and internships include:

www.careerbuilders.com – General job information

www.monster.com – General job information

www.nationjob.com – General job information

www.eco.org – Environmental career opportunities

www.idealist.org – National job information for non-profit corporations

www.execsearches.com – Executives, non-profit positions, and mid-level jobs

www.dice.com – Technical jobs

www.aaas.org – American Association for the Advancement of Science

While a web search can provide valuable information about jobs, it is difficult to determine from a web search just how many job hunters are competing for these jobs.

SELF-EMPLOYMENT

Job hunters, you have made a great deal of progress. You have conducted research and many of you now know the kind of job you are looking for, why this job is a good fit for you, and where to find it.

Some of you may still feel that there really is not a job you can do that fits your personal needs. You may be wondering if self-employment is a good idea.

Is self-employment for you?

Successful small business owners possess these qualities:

1. **Passion** – A strong desire to accomplish a goal or to sell a product or service.

2. **Knowledge of industry** – Whether you are selling a product or a service, you need to know your competition and current business conditions.

3. **Willingness to work long hours and sacrifice paid vacations** – In the beginning, you can expect to never have enough time to get it all done. Although you have complete control, there will be moments in every business when you have to sacrifice some personal time to manage growth, finish jobs, and handle emergencies.

4. **Ability to be flexible** – Entrepreneurs encounter a variety of challenges on a frequent basis. Business plans do not always go as expected, and the ability to be flexible and creative can help sustain your business through the ups and downs of self-employment.

5. **Self-directed** – When you are self-employed, there is no one to tell you to get to work, pat you on the back, or give you feedback. Small business owners must be able to toot their own horn and to manage time and energy effectively.

6. **Good with money** – Cash flow is always a factor in self-employment. Even if your business is going well, the ability to manage and budget your spending, to monitor your accounts payable, and to make wise investments into your business often spells the difference between failure and success.

7. **A history of self-employment** – Persons who have previously been successful in business or who have been previously exposed to a small business (such as through parents or spouses) are more likely to be able to be able to respond positively to the demands of self-employment.

8. **Ability to get along with a wide variety of people** – Although small business owners are able to select the people they hire and work with on a day-to-day basis, small business owners often have to deal with irate customers and unreasonable demands. Instead of having one supervisor at work, small business owners deal with multiple customers, their personalities and priorities, and their corporate values. Be prepared to negotiate.

9. **Sales ability** – Some products and services *do* sell themselves, but all businesses require some level of marketing, selling and closing.

10. **Willingness to set boundaries** – Interruptions affect your concentration, steal your time, and impair your ability to get the job done. Families and friends often feel that because you are self-employed, you are more accessible, so they can call or visit at any time. It can be hard to tell your friends and family that you cannot talk or play now.

Customers may be demanding, slow to pay, or excessively critical. The willingness to set limits, ask for money, and learn from one's mistakes is essential to successful self-employment.

What about partnerships?

Partnerships are tricky. Often, one person ends up doing the majority of the workload; this situation can generate resentments, work delays, and financial problems.

Spouses or families who work with each other may find it difficult to leave their work-related problems at work. They may find that their whole lives revolve around the business, making it difficult to get away from work and have any personal time. Relationships with your partner or family members may not be able to handle the stress of working together so closely and being around each other so frequently.

What are my chances for success?

There are plenty of hidden costs in operating your own business. Overhead, equipment, accounting, postage, paper, taxes, insurance, and computer software charges all add up. Even though you may be charging more per hour than you were previously earning, you may net less money than you would earn in a comparable position with an established company. Although you may not report directly to a boss, you will report instead to many bosses: your customers.

I want to have my own business because I could make twice as much per hour, and I would not have to cater to my boss.

Approximately two-thirds of new businesses survive for two years, and about half survive at least four years.

About one-third of the businesses that close were considered successes and did not close due to "business" failure. Some business (such as restaurants and bars) typically have higher failure rates.

Do your research up front. It may not be necessary to quit your day job or your job search to start your business. Self-employment has risks but also benefits. It is exciting to see your ideas work, the potential for higher earnings is motivating, and the joy of being successful in your own business can make it all worthwhile. Just keep your expectations realistic.

Can I Finance My Business?

Sufficient starting capitol is a critical factor in business startup. The larger the business, the more important it is to have sufficient financing to ensure success. Some small companies may be able to start doing business with very little cash output other than business cards, an occupational license, and a concept.

My father, Edwin Jerome Reuben, a self-taught, successful businessman, taught me to get the customer first, and then buy or hire what you need to get the job done. Of course, this strategy does not work in all businesses, but the concept remains viable. If you buy expensive equipment before you have your first customer, you may find yourself cash-strapped and unable to weather the first year of business.

Before starting a large scale marketing blitz or spending a lot of time hiring and training personnel, try your concept on a small scale. Once you have ironed out some of the inevitable glitches, you can expand. Beware of high startup costs. Try not to invest all of your life savings or use up all of your available credit to start a business.

To find help in developing a business plan, financing, and general information, visit the following websites:

www.sba.gov – Official site of the Small Business Association, a government source devoted to small business development

www.score.org – Service Corps of Retired Executives is a non-profit organization dedicated to providing entrepreneurs with free, confidential, face-to-face and e-mail business counseling. Counseling and workshops are offered at 389 chapter offices across the country.

www.wsj.com – Sponsored by the *Wall Street Journal*, the website offers includes sample business plans, links for venture capitalists, franchising facts, and general information.

FACING THE JOB MARKET

Are you aware that every job hunter in America has legal rights under the Equal Opportunity Employment Act? This law protects against discrimination in hiring.

This chapter explains the common forms of discrimination. You will learn how to best present yourself to all prospective employers to learn all about you–your strengths as well as your weaknesses–in an honest, yet non-discriminatory approach. Your strengths will be recognized. You will see that your strengths are needed in the workplace.

Reasonable accommodations are also discussed in depth and you will have a much better understanding how to accommodate your particular disability in the workplace.

Facing the job market

Facing Workplace Discrimination?

It is illegal for employers to discriminate in hiring people because of race, color, gender, national origin, religion, age, or disability.

Civil rights protection is provided by the
Equal Employment Opportunity Commission (EEOC).

You may be asked some of these *illegal questions*,
which may then be used to *discriminate* against hiring you.

▶ *What is your race?*

▶ *What is your age?*

▶ *Are you married?*

▶ *What is your religious background?*

▶ *Do you have any children?*

▶ *Do you have a back injury?*

▶ *Have you ever been on Workers' Compensation?*

These are some of the other *illegal questions* you may be asked; these questions may be used to *discriminate* against hiring you.

▶ *Are you disabled?*

▶ *Do you take any medications?*

▶ *How many sick days did you take last year?*

▶ *How long have you been handicapped?*

▶ *Why are you in a wheelchair?*

Employers may not ask you questions about your disability, only about your abilities.

You may be asked to <u>voluntarily</u> disclose your disability for affirmative action purposes. (This section is intended only as a guide. Contact the EEOC for specific questions concerning the law and your rights.)

How to Protect Yourself Against Discrimination

Address the concern, not the question!

Some typical concerns or stereotypes regarding older workers:

* May be frequently ill
* May be too old to learn new information
* May be slow
* May not have many work years remaining
* May only want to work part-time
* May take too much time to train

Address the concerns:

If age is the concern, your sample responses may include:

▶ *I am hoping to work for my next company for ten years.*

▶ *I am sure my excellent work experience and years of dependability will be an asset to your company.*

▶ *I am open to learning new information.*

▶ *I am a good listener.*

Typical Concerns and Stereotypes

Some of the typical concerns or stereotypes regarding persons with disabilities :

* May be too difficult or costly to accommodate
* Will drive up health insurance costs
* May re-injure themselves
* Will increase workload on co-worker
* May be frequently absent
* May be dangerous to themselves or others

Address the concerns:

If disability is the concern, your sample responses may include:

▶ *I had a great attendance record at my past job.*

▶ *I might need a little help with _____. Would that be a problem?*

▶ *I am able to perform all of the duties of this job.*

▶ *I can do everything that you described.*

▶ *I do not need health benefits.*

▶ *I have had this disability my whole life and I've had a lot of jobs.*

Some typical concerns or stereotypes regarding family status:

Single Persons
* May not be stable
* May be job-hopping

Single persons with children
* May miss work because of children's illnesses or activities
* Children may come before work

Married
* May be unwilling to travel
* May be unwilling to work long hours

Sample responses:

▶ *I am hoping to grow with a company.*

▶ *I love this area.*

▶ *I have excellent work references.*

▶ *I had 20 sick days to my credit when I left my last job.*

▶ *I am willing to do what it takes to get the job done.*

What If They Ask Me...?

Do you have a back injury?

This question is **NOT** permissible under the Americans with Disability Act. **Address the concern, not the question.**

ADDRESS THE CONCERN. Sample responses:

▶ *Is there something about this job that might be difficult for someone with a back injury?*

▶ *What you do in this job that concerns you?*

▶ *I should not have any trouble working in this position.*

Are you on Workers' Compensation?

This question is **NOT** permissible under the Americans with Disability Act. **Address the concern, not the question.**

ADDRESS THE CONCERN. Sample responses:

▶ *I am currently looking for work.*

▶ *What are you concerned about?*

▶ *I am not sure why you are asking?*

Do you have any children?

This question is **NOT** permissible under the federal anti-discrimination law. **Address the concern, not the question.**

ADDRESS THE CONCERN. Sample responses :

► *Is this a prerequisite for this job?*

► *I have a very dependable work history, and I am free to travel, if that is your concern.*

What is your age?

This question is **NOT** permissible under the federal anti-discrimination law. **Address the concern, not the question.**

ADDRESS THE CONCERN. Sample responses:

► *I am looking for a long-term employment, if that is your concern.*

► *I am a fast learner and still open to new information.*

Can employers ask you about your current medical condition or whether you have had a Workers' Compensation injury?

NO: Any inquiry regarding physical condition is not allowed under the guidelines of the American with Disabilities Act, unless the question specifically **relates** to the **essential functions** of the job.

Can you lift 50 pounds?_____ Yes? _____ No?

This question is allowed, **if the essential functions of the job require the lifting of 50 pounds.** For example, a delivery driver who regularly delivers large packages may be asked that question.

If you are applying for a clerical position, in which **normally there is little lifting,** then this question would **not** be appropriate as the **lifting of 50 pounds is not essential** to the job for which you are applying.

The law requires that employers consider only a person's work qualifications and a person's abilities to perform the job functions of the job. To encourage the hiring of persons with disabilities, the law specifically states that employers may not ask about disabilities until after making a conditional job offer.

What Can Employers Ask?

What if they find out that I am on Workers' Compensation or Social Security? Will I be terminated? Will I be covered by health insurance?

Don't worry about it. The law prohibits discrimination, and your Worker's Compensation status has no relevance to your ability to do the job. Your medical coverage through the employer will be the same as any other new employee.

Can employers require a medical exam?

Yes, *after* a conditional offer of employment has been made.

Any examination must be job-related and necessary for business. It must be given to all conditional hires, and results must be stored in a file separate from your personnel file.

What if they find out I have a medical condition?

As long as your medical condition does not interfere with your ability to perform the essential functions of the job, it cannot by law affect the hiring decision.

If you have a **qualified disability**, employers are required to make a reasonable effort to accommodate your disability.

▶ Can you meet the employer's attendance requirements?

Employers are allowed to ask about your ability to be at work. It is not a disability-related question, and there are many reasons why a person may unable to attend work regularly.

▶ Have you ever been arrested or convicted?

This question is permissible.

▶ Do you currently use illegal drugs?

This question is permissible; the current use of illegal drugs is **not** protected under the Americans with Disabilities Act.

▶ Are you able to perform the essential duties of the job with or without reasonable accommodations?

(If you are unable to answer YES to this question, your job goals should be revised, or you may need help determining reasonable accommodations.)

Accommodations

There are many reasons why people need accommodations. People with physical and mental disabilities are not the only ones who need accommodating. Perhaps there is illness, injury, pregnancy, elder parents who need care or young children with special needs.

While the term 'reasonable accommodations' is only guaranteed for persons with documented disabilities, most solutions can be easily implemented without having to formally involve the employer and risk losing the job.

"Can you demonstrate or tell me how you would perform the job?"

If the employer has **reason to believe** that the applicant will need reasonable accommodations due to an obvious disability (person is in a wheelchair, blind, etc.) or because the applicant has **voluntarily disclosed** that he has a disability, then this question is permissible. Ask to see the job description so you know exactly what the essential job functions are.

What *are* "reasonable accommodations?"

A reasonable accommodation is a modification at the workplace which:

does not pose undue hardship on the employer

allows a person with a qualified disability to perform the essential

functions of the job.

Most accommodations cost less than $200!

Types of Accommodations

▶ Assistance with occasional lifting of heavy objects

▶ A stool or ergonomic chair

▶ Flexible work hours

▶ A change in break schedule

▶ An ergonomic keyboard

▶ Modified non-essential duties

▶ A job coach

▶ Training in written form as well as verbal form

When is the best time to talk about your illness or disability?

It is **not** necessary to talk about your disability at all.

If reasonable accommodations are indicated:

From a legal standpoint: After a conditional job offer, a person should inform the employer if he has a disability so that accommodations can be put in place.

Legally an employer only has to provide 'reasonable accommodations' under the ADA for persons who have a documented disability that has been disclosed to the employer. Practically, most reasonable accommodations can be easily implemented without formally involving the employer or invoking legal sanctions. If you know you will need accommodations on the job, take the lead and research how you can accommodate yourself. Make sure you are prepared on how to get these accommodations. It is not the employer's responsibility to figure it all out.

Do You Need Accommodations?

Ask questions to find out what duties are essential to the job:

▶ *Is there a lot of lifting required on the job?*

▶ *What are the job duties?* (Let them tell you what the job is all about.)

▶ *What kind of person do you hope to hire?*

▶ *What exactly would I be doing?*

▶ *Is there a lot of standing? Is there a stool? Could I bring in a stool?*

▶ *Is this a job that involves a lot of paperwork or is it more hands-on?*

Quantify (get precise numbers):

▶ *Would I be typing all day or an hour at a time?*

▶ *How often would I be lifting batteries?*

▶ *Would you say I would be climbing ladders every day or once a week?*

▶ *How often does the merchandise come in?*

▶ *Would I be making 3 stops a day or 20 stops a day?*

> If the time you need to take off for medical treatments is greater than most employers' normal sick leave, vacation leave, FMLA leave, or paid time off
>
> or
>
> if you need a job where you can work around your medical condition, schooling or family, it may make sense to target employers who regularly hire for seasonal work or contract work.

Focus on industries that have ebbs and flows in their personnel needs:

Accounting or income tax firms – Need increased personnel during tax preparation times and less at other times of year.

Health care industries - Hospitals and doctor's offices have slower times of year when less personnel is needed and more hectic times of the year when more personnel needs to be scheduled, especially in locations with a high flux of tourism or seasonal residents.

School employees – Summers are scheduled off and schools have regular holidays.

Retail businesses and carpet cleaners are busier before holidays and often hire extra personnel

Employment agencies and human resource positions are slower during holiday periods.

Delivery companies - Busier during holidays.

Call Centers - Staffs extra people for holiday ordering

Other industries that have ebbs and flows in their personnel needs:

Mystery Shoppers – This is contract work and does not require a commitment other than the assignment that you accept. A typical assignment is for you to eat out at a restaurant and then document specific information that the employer would like to know, for example: How long did it take to be greeted? How was the quality of service and food?

Food Demonstrators - Grocery stores often hire extra people during the holidays to market specific food items for shoppers to taste test.

Sporting Arenas, Fairgrounds, Special events - Hire extra help during events, including ticket takers, security, concessions and parking lot attendants

Survey Takers - Media and marketing firms will hire persons to gather information about their products or services. This is often times limited work.

Inventory Specialists - Large merchants will hire or subcontract to companies who come in and physically count all the items in the stores.

Pre-screening employers

These are questions that you can ask a prospective employer to find out if you will be able to take time off.

Are there times in your industry that business is usually slower? What do your full time employees generally do during these time periods?

Would it be possible to take additional planned time off during the slow periods of the year in order to tend to personal needs?

I generally like to take off some extra time in December. Would this be a problem?

I have some personal affairs that need attention, and I will need about three weeks off this year. I would be willing to take it as unpaid leave. Is there a time in the year that this would be possible?

It is not necessary to go into details, mention surgeries, medical treatments, etc. In fact, don't!

Many people would like to take some planned time off to visit grandchildren, children at college, take a vacation, or attend to personal business, such as selling a deceased parent's home, taking a prolonged trip, or working on a house project.

Job Sharing

Job Sharing is when one full time position is shared by two employees who coordinate with each other to ensure coverage of the position.

It is possible that a current employee who is pregnant or who has young children might be interested in this type of employment. This is also a nice arrangement for persons with mood disorders. If a person's mood swing is severe, through job sharing, the job is not lost.

The ICCD Clubhouse, www.iccd.org has centers worldwide and one of the ways that they help persons with bipolar and other mood disorders is through job sharing.

Job sharing is for people who need flexibility to stay in the workforce.

Work-at-Home – This option is increasingly possible and one of our nations fastest-growing industries. Persons with disabilities are sometimes unable to work outside of the home because of immune problems, stamina, difficulty with transportation or the need for special accommodations. Work at home jobs make the workplace accessible for persons who traditionally would be unable to work.

While there are many work at home scams on the Internet, there are also many legitimate companies that now have work at home divisions. If it sounds too good to be true, then it probably is a scam. Common scams include companies that need people to assemble products, do data entry, take surveys or stuff envelopes. Rule of thumb is that if you have to pay to get started, it is most likely a scam.

There are two types of work from home employment: Contract worker and employee. Contract workers (1099 employees) pay their own taxes and usually can set their own hours. These types of jobs may be long-term or short-term employment.

Some common contract jobs include computer programming, web design, project management, writing, and medical transcriptions.

The other way people get hired is as a company employee. Many companies offer full benefits for their work at home employees, including health insurance, vacations and sick days. Companies that take a lot of customer service calls, such as telephone companies, computer software and hardware manufacturers, credit card companies, retail stores and cable companies often partner with companies that manage their call center operations.

Using the Job Description to Determine the Need for Accommodations

Job descriptions are not required by law, but most employers have something in writing that describes their jobs. Government agencies and public institutions always have job descriptions. They are often published on the Internet or can be obtained in print from the human resources department. Most large employers also publish job descriptions.

> **Job descriptions usually include the following items:**
> 1. Primary job functions
> 2. Minimum educational requirements
> 3. Number of years of work experience desired

Some employers will list the actual physical and emotional requirements of the job; for other jobs, you will need to read "between the lines."

Some job descriptions indicate that applicants must be able to pass a background check, which might be a screening for a criminal history or for your credit history.

Licenses, credentials, or certifications needed for the job are usually listed.

A clear job description is helpful not only for the applicant but also for the interviewer. It is easier to be objective about whether or not a person can do the job (or do it well) when the job duties are clearly defined.

Performance-based interviewing is used by many employers to ensure compliance with the American with Disabilities Act and fairness in hiring. Performance-based interviewing addresses each area of job duties in a highly structured interviewing process.

> Just because something is written on a job description does not mean that it is necessarily an essential requirement of a job.

In the next section, we will look at specific job descriptions for real positions. Read these descriptions to determine what the actual job duties are and what accommodations might be required. ☞

Using the Job Description to Identify Job Duties

Below are two examples of job descriptions that describe the physical, mental and emotional requirements.

| Presto Dry Cleaners | Dry Cleaner Counter Worker |

Nature of Work:

Greet customers; receive, tag, and sort laundry by type, fabric, and color; deliver finished products to customer; take payment.

Job Functions:

In-person and telephonic customer service answering customer questions and providing routine information

Walk to customer's car and carry in laundry products

Handle and shake out laundry to sort and bundle

Enter orders into computer and write names on tickets

Staple and tear tags to identify work orders

Inspect pockets and mark clothes for missing buttons and for stains

Retrieve finished laundry from racks and receive payment from customers using cash register and POS system

Count money at end of shift and complete related paperwork

May assemble cleaned products and perform other laundry-related work

Experience required: Prefers 1 year of customer service experience

Minimum Qualifications: Graduation from high school or possession of a G.E.D. certificate; or an equivalent combination of education, training and/or experience.

Physical Activities and Requirements:

Must be able to stand for up to 7 hours a day

Must be able to walk on a frequent basis

Must be able to lift overhead up to 15 pounds on a frequent basis

Must be able to grip and handle on a frequent basis

Must be able to read and write work orders in English

Must be able to hear average or normal conversations

Must be able to talk and convey information accurately, loudly, or quickly

Emotional and Mental Activities and Requirements:

Use arithmetic to total costs and make change

Establish and maintain effective working relationships with customers and co-workers

Operations Manager

Nature of Work:

This is supervisory work managing laundry personnel and workflow to ensure a profitable and quality dry-cleaning operation.

Job Functions:

Supervise and coordinate activities of counter workers, drivers, pressers, shirt assemblers and laundry workers engaged in receiving, marking, washing, delivering, and pressing clothes or linen in laundry.

Schedule, prioritize, and manage workflow and personnel to provide quick and efficient service to customers and to regulate workload. Reassigns personnel stations as indicated. Set up daily bank in cash register and close out counter cashiers.

Physically inspect machines and work environment to ensure safety. Observe operation of machines and equipment to detect possible malfunctions. Inspect finished products to ensure conformance to standards. Assist workers with tasks as needed. Investigate and resolve customer complaints. Perform related work as assigned or required.

Prefers: Bachelor's Degree in Management or related field and 2 years experience in dry cleaning operations; or an equivalent combination of education, training, and/or experience

Physical Activities and Requirements:

Must be able to stand and walk for 8 hours a day

Must be able to grip and handle on an occasional basis

Must be able to lift up to 20 pounds on an occasional basis

Must be able to reach overhead and lift up to 5 pounds

Must be able to read and write work orders in English

Must be able to hear average or normal conversations

Must be able to talk and convey information accurately, loudly, or quickly

Must be able to tolerate humid and hot atmospheric conditions

Emotional and Mental Activities and Requirements:

Ability to communicate in complex sentences, using normal word order with present, past and future tenses

Compute discount, interest, profit, and loss, and commissions from piecework

Read safety rules and instructions in the use and maintenance of shop tools and equipment; understand and maintain MSDS requirements

Ability to remain professional and thorough under stressful situations and to maintain focus in an environment with frequent interruptions

Using the Job Description to Determine Essential Functions

> (On this job description, the employer is not precise in regards to physical and emotional requirements, but the work duties are clearly detailed.)

*ENVIRONMENTAL SPECIALIST
> 02428
> ### Nature of Work
> This is technical field and office work in an environmental land use management, air, water, or groundwater pollution control program. This is entry level for the Environmental Specialist career ladder. Promotion to the next level will be determined by satisfying established criteria.

> Work involves assisting in a wide variety of tasks, including environmental inspection, enforcement details, monitoring, sampling, evaluation, and analysis related to the protection of the County's natural resources. Work involves the enforcement of national, state and local environmental laws, ordinances, codes, and regulations. Duties may include site development plan review, field investigations, permit issuance, collection of air or water samples for monitoring pollutants, environmental impact assessments, investigation of potential environmental hazards, calculation of retention and drainage, preparation of environmental reports, and inspections for certificates of compliance. Employee may deal with hazardous or toxic pollutants.

> Assignments are made orally or in writing, and work is reviewed through observation of results obtained, conferences, and periodic reports or evaluations.

> ### Illustrative tasks
>> Reviews site development plans and permit applications, conducts field investigations for compliance with environmental codes and ordinances, recommends modifications to ensure regulatory compliance, and inspects sites for certificates of compliance with approved site development plans.
>> Performs field inspections and makes recommendations and limited decisions on the removal of protected vegetation; issues permits.
>> Prepares and serves fine citations and may appear in court as a witness.
>> Assists businesses, contractors, developers, engineers, and the public with interpretation of environmental regulations and compliance with federal, state, and local environmental laws, codes and ordinances.
>> Conducts sampling and field investigations for air or water quality programs, including the operation, calibration, and routine maintenance of specialized sampling apparatus and pollution control testing and monitoring equipment.
>> Collects and maintains technical environmental data, interprets the results of laboratory tests, evaluates ecological and environmental impact, and develops reports on specialized studies.

> From the review of job tasks, it would appear that the employee would have to be able to walk on uneven ground to collect environmental data. The amount of lifting required is not apparent.

Performs quality assurance tests and audits, validating the integrity of environmental data, and performs technical statistical analyses of data using automated programs.

Evaluates conformance with established environmental codes, ordinances and regulations and initiates field enforcement actions based on inspection findings of administrative or operational non-compliance.

Conducts permitting reviews and special assessments on mangroves, wetlands, and uplands to protect environmentally sensitive areas.

Investigates citizen complaints on land use, air or water quality matters, including fish kills, noxious odors, hazardous waste, etc.

Performs related work as assigned or required.

Knowledge, Skills and Abilities

Basic knowledge of environmentally-related codes, laws, rules, ordinances and regulations, and the principles of environmental pollution control.

Knowledge of mathematics and natural, physical, and biological sciences.

Knowledge of scientific research techniques, including the collection of sampling data and preparation of environmental reports.

Ability to read and interpret blueprints, plats, maps, aerial photos, and diagrams.

Ability to operate, calibrate, and perform routine maintenance and repair on assigned electronic and mechanical environmental monitoring equipment.

Ability to formulate and present ideas and findings clearly and concisely in written, oral, or graphic form.

Ability to operate basic computerized data analysis equipment.

Ability to swim and operate small watercraft may be required based upon area of assignment.

Ability to testify in court as an expert witness. ⟵ *Requires a high level of emotional control*

Minimum Qualifications

Must have driver's license and physically be able to drive ⟶ Graduation from an accredited four (4) year college or university with major course work in environmental, physical, natural, or biological science, engineering, or related field; or an equivalent combination of education, training and/or experience.

Possession and maintenance of a valid Florida Driver's License.

Depending upon area of assignment, the employee may be required to be a non-smoker and submit to periodic physical examinations for medical monitoring.

If another employee can take the swimming assignments, the employer may be able to accommodate an applicant who cannot swim.

While driving is listed as a minimum requirement of the job, it may not be an *essential* requirement. For example, Joe had been working as an environmental tech for three years when he developed epilepsy and had a *grand mal* seizure. The doctor would not allow him to drive. If his other job duties will not endanger him or others if he has a seizure, and if there are other people working in his crew that can drive, the employer may be able to accommodate him.

Can the Employer Physically Accommodate You?

POSITION: Wiring, Assembly

COMPANY: Grande Staffing

SALARY: $11-12/hour

DESCRIPTION: 2-3 immediate openings!! Recent technical or vocational graduates are encouraged to apply. Will be refurbishing generators. Work will include wiring point-to-point from wiring diagrams. Must be able to use hand tools to modify aluminum or steel cabinets for new/changed components. Must be able to determine component layouts from drawings or sketches, mark drilling details on surfaces to be modified, drill and tap holes, install components using mechanical fasteners and hand tools. Must be able to distinguish colors of wires for color coding and read wiring diagrams.

Ask questions, like the questions below, to address any concerns that you might have about the job requirements:

▶ *What type of generators would you be repairing? Are they large or are they small?*

▶ *Most of the time, would I be sitting or standing?*

▶ *Would I be working on a assembly line or would I be working on one generator at a time?*

▶ *Would there be a lot of walking involved?*

▶ *Would you consider hiring someone who is not fluent in English?*

▶ *Is this repetitive work or are there a variety of duties?*

▶ *Would a person have to have good hearing?*

ASSEMBLY TECHNICIAN
Precise Electronics is seeking a skilled Assembly Technician

Education Requirements: AS degree in Electronics

Experience Requirements: Minimum of 2 years experience in equipment maintenance/repair (preferably semiconductor industry).

Job Responsibilities: Perform preventive and corrective maintenance on equipment.

Responsible for troubleshooting and repair of minor mechanical, electrical/electronic and pneumatic tool issues.

Follow area-documented procedures for maintenance and troubleshooting. Support and suggest documentation improvements and modifications.

Work in a team environment that supports Manufacturing and works directly with suppliers/vendors.

Must have a strong desire to learn with the ability and aptitude to continually improve and repair increasingly complex issues.

Minimum Requirements: 2 years experience

Languages: English

Ask questions, like these, to address concerns you might have about the job requirements:

► *Would I be primarily sitting or standing?*

► *Would you consider work experience in lieu of education?*

► *Would there be a lot of walking involved?*

► *Is this heavy work?*

► *Do you use a lot of chemicals in your factory?*

As you can see, the physical, emotional and mental requirements of assembly positions vary greatly depending on the company.

While being able to communicate in English seems to be important at Precise Electronics, English skills probably would not be as important at the job through Grande staffing.

While you do not want to draw too much attention to your concerns, it is a good idea to ask questions about a job to determine if the job would be right for you.

REED SERVICES

Office Assistant

Performs general clerical tasks. Operates basic office equipment. Sorts and routes incoming materials. May require computer and data entry skills.

Employers' job descriptions are not always very detailed. Ask questions to find out exactly what your would be doing.

▶ *Would I be typing most of the time or are there a variety of duties?*

▶ *What typing speed are you looking for?*

▶ *How many hours a day would I be typing?*

▶ *How much computer experience do you need?*

▶ *Would I be answering phones?*

▶ *How many people work there?*

▶ *Would I be working with customers?*

▶ *Do the job duties vary from day to day or are they pretty routine in nature?*

▶ *Is this a fast-paced job?*

So you get the idea...

If repetitive typing is a problem — **Quantify, Quantify, Quantify** — find out how much typing is required on an average day.

If you are not good with customers, **ask questions** to find out if you would be handling customers.

If you do not work well with others, **find out** if you would be working with a large staff or if it is a one-person office.

If you are unable to work fast, **ask** the employer about the pace of the job.

**Digital Communications Dispatcher
Non Standard Hours**
Class Code 2773-0

Note: The following duties are illustrative and not exhaustive. The omission of specific statements of duties does not exclude them from the position if the work is similar, related, or a logical assignment to the position. Depending on assigned area of responsibility, incumbents in the position may perform some or all of the activities described below.

1-Receives telephone calls from citizens requesting emergency assistance; screens the calls and initiates appropriate action.

2-Operates digital and audio communications equipment to dispatch law enforcement assistance, emergency medical vehicles, or fire units.

3-Maintains records such as shift reports, operational logs, and equipment availability.

4-Performs other related duties as required.

Minimum Qualifications (Must Be Attained Before the Recruitment Ending Date):

Graduation from high school or possession of a GED certificate; and a passing score on a written test; and a passing score on a data entry test at 100 gross keystrokes per minute with 90% accuracy.

Special Probationary Note:

Initial employment with the Sheriff's Office will be in a trainee status for approximately 3 - 6 months, based on individual performance.

Appointing Authority May Require

Possession of a current Driver License.

(job description continues on page 143)

Do you see any reason why someone who uses a wheelchair could not work in this job?

Special Note
All selected applicants for employment at Hillsborough County Aviation Authority must successfully pass a fingerprint-based FBI criminal history check in accordance with Federal Aviation Regulation, Part 107.209.

Veterans' Preference
Preference in initial appointment will be given to eligible veterans and eligible spouses of veterans. Documentation to support entitlement to preference MUST be provided at the time of application.

Note
Depending on the agency of employment, individuals hired may be required to review Hillsborough County driving eligibility criteria and acknowledge their understanding of its provisions.

Notice
The employers of Hillsborough County have implemented a drug-free workplace and all offers of employment are conditioned on job applicants successfully passing a drug test.

Examination
Examination may be administered at the time of application or scheduled at a later date. Test information is available at the Reception Branch, Hillsborough County Civil Service Office. This information must be obtained in person and it is the applicant's responsibility to obtain it, if desired.

Recruitment Period
This recruitment has been in progress for two weeks. It is now being extended as of March 24, 1999, and may be withdrawn at any time.

> **A person who had a poor criminal history could probably not be accommodated, as emergency dispatcher is a position that involves a high degree of trust and responsibility.**
>
> **A person who is emotionally unable to handle emergency situations would also not be a good candidate for this position.**

Using a Job Analysis to Determine Job Demands

A *job analysis* is a tool that is used to determine physical or emotional functions of a job. For legal purposes, a job analysis is often performed by a certified vocational evaluator, certified job analyst, or certified rehabilitation counselor. For informational purposes or for the purpose of developing a thorough job description, a job analysis may be conducted by any conscientious person. *These are examples.*

Job Analysis

MILTON MACHINE SHOP

Job Title: Machinist

Job Duties: Operate machine that manufactures cutters; deburr metal pieces as they come out of the machine

Exertion Level:

▶ Alternates standing, sitting, and walking

▶ Lifts metal pieces, weighing from 5-50# - (size is like a round weight for a weight-lifting machine) from ground level up to waist level (requires squatting)

▶ Places metal piece on cart and pushes cart about 50 ft into other room

▶ Lifts piece to chest level and inserts it into machine

▶ Tightens weight to machine using Allen wrench

▶ Pushes button to start machine

▶ Watches machine that grinds and cuts, adjusting water jets as needed

▶ Takes weight off of machine and places it on table for deburring

▶ Using hand file, files off rough edges

Work Level: Semi-skilled

Special Comments: Engine hoists are available to lift metal parts
Reviewed by: Paula Vieillet, CVE, July 13, 2008

This job analysis was conducted on behalf of a person who has a back problem to determine whether or not he would be able to work as a machinist. As Bob's physical requirements included the ability to change positions frequently, and as he was restricted to no lifting over 50 pounds, it appeared that this position would be an appropriate career direction.

As Bob did not have any formal machinist background, and retraining was indicated, the job analysis was helpful in determining whether or not he should enter the machinist program. To ensure the ability to secure competitive employment, other machine shops were also contacted. (Physical requirements will vary from shop to shop.)

Elextronics

Job Title: Kit Assembler

Job Duties: Make kits for assembly department by retrieving small plastic or metal parts from shelves; puts specified number and types of parts in bag; seals bag; carries box and places on shelf in assembly room.

Exertion Level:

▶ Standing, walking

▶ Takes parts out of boxes or bags (less than 3 lbs.) and weighs parts on scale

▶ Weighs parts on table scale to determine number of parts

▶ Pours small parts from bowl on scale into a hard plastic bag

▶ Seal bag using sealer (operates by pushing down on lever; little force required)

▶ May bend to reach parts stored on lower shelves

▶ May reach overhead to reach parts stored on higher shelves

▶ May occasionally climb stepladder (has side rails; ladder automatically locks in position when stepped on to reach parts on high shelves)

▶ Carries box of finished assembly kit into assembly room (would generally be less than 5 lbs.; can get assistance if necessary)

Work Level: This job is generally learned in a very short time; no formal training required.

Comments: Although there was frequent handling, the handling was not repetitive in nature.

Reviewed by: Signature_____

Paula Vieillet, MA, Certified Vocational Evaluator, July 28, 2008

> This job analysis was initiated at the request of the employer's Worker's Compensation Insurance Carrier, to determine whether or not an employee with limitations on repetitive handling and lifting could return to work in this position.
>
> A copy of this job analysis was sent to the employee's physician with a request to review the job analysis and make a determination as to whether or not the person could physically perform in this position.
>
> This is a common practice that insurance companies use to quantify a person's ability to return to work.

What if I get the job and find out that there is more lifting or typing involved than disclosed in the interview or on the job description?

You are covered under the Americans with Disabilities Act, whether you are working or not. If you find that you need help with accommodations, either prior to your becoming employed or when you are working, you can call a toll-free national hotline:

Jobs Accommodations (JAN) 1-800-526-7234

Internet address : **www.jan.wvu.edu**

This is a free consulting service that provides information on available aids, devices and methods for accommodating workers with disabilities.

Other resources include :

NARIC - National Rehabilitation Information Center
8455 Colesville Rd.
Silver Spring, MD 20910
1-800-346-2742

Internet address : www.naric.com

This organization has an extensive web site providing information related to disability, including a library of current and prospective research projects, funding for rehabilitation projects and a database of over 60,000 publications of literature on disability.

Assistance for Persons With Different Abilities

Where to Report Discrimination:

The Equal Employment Employment Commission has fair practice centers nationwide to register complaints and encourage compliance:

Call 1-800-669-3362 for written information

or

visit them on the Web at: **http://www.eeoc.gov**

Your Personal Accommodations

Write out your own answers to these questions:

What accommodations will you most probably need?

(Examples: stool, ergonomic keyboard or chair, change in break schedule, help with lifting heavy objects)

Where or how can they be obtained?

(Examples: Be specific. What store or catalog sells what you need?)

How much do they cost?

Who will provide these accommodations? Whom do I need to ask?

(Example: Prospective employer, rehabilitation agency, insurance company, self)

From a legal standpoint: Employer pays for accommodations (except for personal items like glasses, wheelchair, hearing aid, etc.).

From a practical standpoint: You might consider other resources beyond your employer or, if you can and it is easier, pay for them yourself.

How To Suggest Accommodations

If you need special accommodations for any type of disability/different ability, below are listed some possible ways to go about suggesting these accommodations to a new or prospective employer:

▶ Do you think it would be okay if I arranged my time a little differently? Could I do some typing for an hour and then some filing?

▶ It is difficult for me to climb ladders. Would you be able to schedule someone else on the jobs that require climbing a ladder?

▶ Since the truck comes in on Wednesdays, would you be able to schedule my day off on Wednesdays? I have difficulty physically carrying more than 25 pounds, and it sounds like this day would involve a lot of lifting.

▶ It sounds like I have exactly the qualifications you are looking for to fill the position, but it would be easier for me if I could work flexible hours. Would that be possible?

▶ I would love to work here, but I am unable to stand all day. Would it be possible to use a stool during part of the time?

▶ If there are accommodations which are possible but a little inconvenient, try to assist the employer by demonstrating how you would be able to function at the job.

> ### Sometimes, employers will *not* be able to accommodate you.
>
> **For example:** A stool may present a safety hazard, or the company is small and they do not have anybody who can help. It is not always reasonable for employers to modify jobs.
>
> **Thank them, ask for a referral, and keep looking!**

Now that you know yourself better, and you know what technologies and accommodations might help you at work, you probably have a career in mind.

List your job goal(s).

1.

2.

3.

What still worries you about working in these jobs?

What accommodations might be helpful?

What would you like to find out about these jobs?

Job Search

You probably now have a few jobs in mind that you would like to learn more about. Perhaps you would even like to try working at these jobs.

You may not know whether or not an employer can make accommodations for you, or whether or not they do much hiring. You still may not know if the job would really suit you.

By talking to people who currently work in your areas of interest, you can learn more about the field and its hiring practices. The more you know, the more prepared you will be for a job interview.

In fact, while you are exploring careers by actively talking to people about their jobs, you never know, you might run across a job opening waiting for the right person — YOU!

Tell Me About Your Job

THE YELLOW PAGES APPROACH

Use the Yellow Pages or **www.yellowpages.com** to identify companies that hire people with your job goal. For example, if your job goal is to work as a receptionist in a veterinary clinic, start calling veterinarian offices, and ask them if they are hiring. Use this sample script:

"Hi, my name is _____. I'm calling to see if you are doing any hiring for a _____ ?" (Use the title of a specific job.)

If the answer is *yes*, ask the following :

▶   *What are you looking for?*

Listen carefully and ask appropriate questions like:

▶ *Is the job very physical?*

▶ *Is there a lot of walking?*

▶ *Is there a lot of lifting?*

Ask questions to determine the primary duties of the job, and to address any concerns you may have with this particular type of job.

Ask specific questions relating to work conditions.

If the job is suitable, say:

▶ *I am very interested in this position.*

▶ *I have experience* (describe in a short sentence) *and this is exactly the type of work that I am looking for.*

▶ *Would it be possible for me to talk to you in person? I could come in this afternoon or tomorrow.*
("Tomorrow would be fine.")

Would 9:00 a.m. be a good time to come?
("9:00 a.m. would be perfect. See you then!")

THE YELLOW PAGES APPROACH

This person was interested in finding out more about the field of prosthetics technician. He had physical limitations that involved limited standing and limited manipulation with his right hand. He called a prosthetics manufacturer who was listed in the Yellow Pages.

"My name is James Smith. I'm interested in finding out about the field of prosthetics technician. Do you ever hire people for this position?

("Yes, on occasion.")

"I wanted to find out a little more about the actual job duties."

("I think you might need to speak to the manager about that. I handle the office.")

"What is the manager's name?"

("Jim.")

"Is he available?"

("I'll transfer you.")

"I'm interested in finding out about the field of prosthetics technician. I was wondering what the techs really do. Would you mind sharing a bit of time to talk to me?"

("The techs are responsible for manufacturing the frame and hardware of the prosthetics. They work with molds, stains, and other building materials.")

I was wondering a little about the physical requirements of the job. Is it very physical?

("No, not really. It is mostly mechanical bench work and fabrication.")

What kind of people do well in this job?

("People with construction and manufacturing background often do well, as this job involves working with plaster and other materials used in these fields.")

(continued ☞)

THE YELLOW PAGES APPROACH

"Are you currently hiring?"
> ("We might consider bringing someone on.")

"Do you ever train?"
> ("Yes, we do.")

"I would love to come by and see exactly what a prosthetics technician does before I jump into the field. Would it be possible for me to stop by for a couple of minutes?"
> ("That would be fine.")

"Would tomorrow be a good time or would Wednesday be better?"
> ("Wednesday would be better.")

"Okay, Wednesday. How about 10:00 a.m.?"
> ("Afternoon would be better.")

"What time is good for you?"
> ("Let's say 3:00 p.m.")

"Great, 3:00 p.m. is perfect. I'll see you on Wednesday."

THE PERSONAL & NETWORKING APPROACH

What is networking?

Networking is another word for connecting with people. The word "networking" is fairly new, but the concept of networking has been around since cavemen.

Back when cavemen networked, they probably shared tips on how they made a fire or they showed off their latest hunting tool. Usually networking involves meeting people with a specific goal in mind. Many people believe networking involves asking your friends for a job. This is simply not true.

Is networking better than answering ads?

Did you know that only about 30% of jobs are advertised! Most jobs are found through word-of-mouth, staffing or executive search firms, or by directly contacting employers likely to hire you.

So how do I get started networking?

Really, anywhere is fine. The more you talk to people about their work and their places of employment, the closer you are to your next job.

Networking is similar to socializing because networking involves meeting new people and keeping up with previous co-workers and friends, except that when you network for a job, you remain focused on your goal of getting a job, learning about a new career field, or getting a better job! Facebook and Linked-In are great ways to reconnect.

I talk to people already. But no one has ever told me about a job opening!
You must bring it up.

▶ *Where you work, do they ever do any hiring for* (insert your job goal) *?*

▶ *Do you know anyone who works in my field?*

▶ *I would love to learn more about a career in* (insert your career goal)

▶ *Do you know anyone who works in* (that field) *who might not mind talking with me*?

THE PERSONAL & NETWORKING APPROACH

Many people are shy when it comes to asking others if they know of any jobs and feel that they are imposing when talking to others about their jobs.

> **The truth is most people love to talk about their jobs.**

In fact, in America – unlike other countries – it is customary when you meet someone new at a party or at a gathering to ask, "**What do you do?**"

How do you answer the question 'What do you do' when you are out of work? This question sends chills to many job hunters and can evoke feelings of shame or inferiority.

Try a little humor!

▶ *"I am a professional job hunter. What do you do?"*

▶ *"I'm a highly skilled job hunter. What do you do?"*

▶ *"I am a career specialist, always looking for something new. What do you do?"*

How do you answer the question 'What do you do' when you are under-employed or in a low-paying job?

Again, use humor if appropriate.

▶ *Selling myself cheap! What do you do?*

▶ *I am working there until I can find something in my field.*

▶ *A paycheck is better than no paycheck.*

▶ *I am trying to better myself. What do you do?*

THE PERSONAL & NETWORKING APPROACH

Although the goal of networking is to get interviews, people you are talking to will not be motivated to help you until *you have established some connection with them.*

Again, most people love talking about their jobs *except* when they are having some trouble on their job or when they work in a profession that involves advising or counseling people, such as doctors and lawyers. Even then, as long as you ask questions related to finding out more about the profession, and you refrain from questions that would be more appropriately answered at their job, most people are more than happy to share their career experiences.

> **When you listen and ask appropriate questions, you are <u>demonstrating</u> that you are a good listener.**

When networking, if you meet resistance from people, you may want to lighten up and take a less direct approach. Try making a connection on any topic.
Below are some possible examples:

► *Why are you here today?*

► *How do you know the host/hostess?*

► *Have you been coming here for a long time?*

► *Do you know many people here?*

► *I love that painting; what do you think?*

Beware of spending too much time helping others or just chatting with people. *Your needs are just as important as the other person's needs.* Be sure to mention, at some point, that you are looking for a job.

> Good listening and communication skills are important in almost every career.
>
> A person who listens and communicates well off-the-job will also listen well on-the-job.

If you still feel uncomfortable with networking, re-read this chapter and practice *changing your thoughts.*

Being without paid employment or being under-employed may be stressful, but it does NOT make you inferior.

You are just a person who is in-between jobs or who wants a better job.

Remember, most people have periods in their lives when they are unemployed or under-employed.

I am not the kind of person who just talks to people in grocery store lines or at the park. What are some other good ways to network?

1. Call previous co-workers or work acquaintances:

"Hi Jerry, how are you doing? How are things at XYZ company? You know that job I took at ABC corporation?"

▶ *"Well, it did not work out for me."*

▶ *"Did you know ABC is going bankrupt."*

▶ *"Their jobs went overseas."*

▶ *"They didn't appreciate my talents. Remember how we worked together on...."*

  (or, make some other reference that reminds them of your specific skills and

  abilities).

Keeping up contact with old contacts *can be your ticket to your next job* OR *it may be their ticket to their next job.* Remember, it goes both ways. Staying connected is a good way to find a job fast.

2. Join your trade or professional association. Get active and join a committee:

If you do not know if there is an association in your field, the local Yellow Pages is a good place to start. Look under "Associations." You will be amazed at the abundance and variety of associations. You can also research national associations on the Internet. Just type in your occupation and "association" in any search engine.

Even if you can barely afford the membership dues, it is worth joining. Just think how expensive it is for you to be unemployed! Many professional associations list job openings for their members. Staying active with your association also keeps you from becoming isolated and outdated in your field.

THE PERSONAL APPROACH

3. Join any association.

Again, the Yellow Pages is a good place to start. Join any club that will bring you into contact with positive people: Kiwanis Club, the Shriners, an Hispanic association, your condominium association, the Junior League, a civic association, or wherever your heart takes you.

Toastmasters International

I am particularly partial to Toastmasters International. Its goal is to help people improve their communication and leadership skills.

By joining Toastmasters International, you will learn how to speak extemporaneously on a variety of subjects. At the beginning of every meeting, there is a "Table Topics" time when each member has the opportunity to give a two-minute reply to a question posed by the "Table Topic Master."

This is great training for interviews! Even though the questions will be different in an interview, you will grow more comfortable and become more skilled at speaking without preparation, on a variety of topics. At job interviews you are usually asked at least one or two questions that you did not anticipate.

Another reason for joining Toastmasters International is that more people will have an opportunity to get to know you—the real you—and you will grow more comfortable speaking about yourself and in public.

The leadership aspect of Toastmasters International will help you develop leadership skills, even if you have never worked in management. Again, these skills are highly prized in almost any type of work environment.

All kinds of people join Toastmasters. You do not require qualifications of any kind except a willingness to learn and grow. Toastmasters is a great way to boost your confidence level and self-esteem, and it looks good on any resume.

Go to **www.toastmasters.org** or
look in your community newspaper or
Yellow Pages for local information.

THE PERSONAL APPROACH

4. Volunteer

Volunteering is an excellent way to get to know people. Perhaps you could volunteer at your local hospital, humane society, food pantry, your children's school or sports team, a museum, Habitat for Humanity, community events, or wherever your heart takes you and volunteer opportunities are available in all kinds of fields.

I especially recommend volunteering if you want to work at a job where they use volunteers. A good friend of mine, a breast cancer survivor, volunteered to be a speaker. She now works in a full-time, paid position for the National Cancer Society as a speaker and a coordinator for major funding and educational events.

5. Attend your church, synagogue, mosque, spiritual group, or support group.

No matter what your faith, spiritual beliefs or personal challenges, there are other people whose beliefs and challenges are similar to yours.

By joining with others like yourself, you will feel a greater sense of connectedness and less isolation. You may hear something that makes your day go a little easier or even meet someone whose company is hiring.

Twelve-step groups are a proven, safe and effective method for people with challenges. Alcoholics Anonymous, Al-Anon (a group for families and friends of alcoholics), Gamblers Anonymous, Overeaters Anonymous, and Obsessive Compulsive Anonymous are just a few of the support groups that can help you feel better about yourself and give you the opportunity to meet new people.

> Remember, when you are networking for a job and meeting new people, do not forget to ask if their company is hiring or if they know someone that you could talk to who works in your field.

THE PERSONAL APPROACH

My network is paying off. My acquaintance said his company is hiring!

Say something like this: *"Sounds like it is a pretty good company to work for! I don't know if I mentioned it to you, but I'm looking at job opportunities and this sounds pretty interesting."*

Get the name of the person you need to talk with. This might be the department manager, the foreman, the human resource director, or the person in the next office.

▶ *Who would I need to talk to?*

▶ *Would you mind if I said that you referred me?*

Thank your acquaintance and follow-up!

What if my acquaintance says that he or she is the person who does the hiring? Should I ask if he or she would hire me?

No. Hold off until the person has a chance to formally interview you. Instead, mention that you would love to talk further about the position. *Give the person a choice.*

▶ *Would tomorrow be a good time for me to call on you?*

▶ *Would morning or afternoon be better?*

(Possible response: *"Neither. How about Monday or Tuesday?"*)

This is a proven sales technique. Be assertive but not pushy. If the person seems unwilling or unavailable to meet with you, ask if he or she would mind looking at your resume; fax or email it to them the very next morning.

Does this mean that I will get hired if I meet someone through networking?

No. You still need to ask "*Are they hiring where you work?*" and you still need to be a good fit for the job. However, networking does greatly improve your chances of getting hired! Jobs that are not advertised get fewer applicants than jobs that *are* advertised, so you may have less competition.

NETWORKING

You are doing a great job of networking!

 Check all that apply:

❑ You demonstrated initiative.

❑ You demonstrated the ability to gather important information.

❑ You were able to form or strengthen a relationship.

❑ You were able to share your skills with another person.

❑ You had the opportunity to show others that you have considerable knowledge about a particular field or industry.

❑ You were able to be direct and ask for what you need.

❑ When you followed up as agreed, you demonstrated reliability.

Even if you do not meet anyone this time, next time might just be your lucky day.

> **Personal contact: Whether you do it by telephone, in person, or in following up an Internet job lead, personal contact is the most effective method.**
>
> **People hire people.**

I will prepare and some day my chance will come.

—Abraham Lincoln

ON YOUR MARK!
GET SET! GO. . .

Review and practice of this section will help you to master the application, interviewing, and follow-up processes.

It will be helpful for you to complete the practice application and contact your references, letting them know you are in the process of job hunting. It also helps to run through a mock interview, using your customized sample responses with someone else asking you the sample questions. This will reinforce your learning process.

Be sure to follow-up after you have applied with a company. It reminds the employer that you are interested in the job.

As you start working, remember that your employer was willing and able to make reasonable accommodations. It is okay if there are some things that you are unable to do. Get help if you need to. You are worth it. You have a lot to offer.

On Your Mark, Set, GO!

Employment Options

APPLICATION FOR EMPLOYMENT
Pre-Employment Questionnaire
Equal Opportunity Employer

Personal Information		Date	2-15-2008	

NAME (Last Name First) Nancy Claxton		Social Security No. 500-02-5421		

Present Address 534 Midland Blvd.	City Memphis		State Tenn	Zip Code 59300
Previous Address	City		State	Zip Code

Phone Number (Home) (810) 734-9488	Phone Number (Cell) (810) 555-9888	Referred By

Position/Employment Desired	Date You Can Start Need time for doctor appointment	Salary Desired

Are You Employed? __X__Yes ____No
If yes, may we inquire of your present employer? ____Yes ____No

Have you ever applied to this company before? ____Yes __X__ No
If yes, where?   When?

NAME AND LOCATION OF SCHOOL	YEARS ATTENDED
High School East Lake High School	4
College	
Trade, Business, or Correspondence School	

SUBJECTS OF SPECIAL STUDY/RESEARCH

CERTIFICATIONS
US MILITARY   RANK
SPECIAL INTERESTS

FORMER EMPLOYERS (List last four, starting with the most recent first.)

MONTH/YEAR	NAME & ADDRESS	POSITION	SALARY	REASON
11/1999– 2/2002	AMD Hospital	CNA	$10.75	Worker's Comp Injury
08/1994—6/1995	Beech Industries	Quality Control	$6.85	Left to take care of children
3/1994—5/1994	McDonalds	Fast Food	$6.50	Fired

SPECIAL QUALIFICATIONS (PLEASE LIST)

_____

_____

ARE YOU AUTHORIZED TO WORK IN THE UNITED STATES? _____YES _____NO

(NOTE: If you are hired, you wil be required to submit proof of legal right to work in the United States.)

CAN YOU PERFORM THE JOB WITH OR WITHOUT REASONABLE ACCOMMODATIONS? _____YES ____X____NO (Can't do any lifting.)

HAVE YOU EVER BEEN CONVICTED OF A FELONY? _____YES ___X___NO

(NOTE: If yes, please explain)

REFERENCES: Give below the names of three persons not related to you, whom you have known at least one year. (Would you hire this person?)

NAME	ADDRESS	TELEPHONE NUMBER	BUSINESS	YEARS KNOWN
1. Jill Thompson	Memphis	(836) 355-1077	Retired	16
2. Bob Claxton	3549 Drew St.	(810) 734-9488	Carpenter	Whole Life
3. Mary Briggs	Lee County Social Services	(810) 321-9087	Caseworker	4

AGREEMENT: (Please read following statements carefully).

I certify that all information on this application and any other material provided by me is true and complete. I agree that falsified information on this application shall be grounds for dismissal.

I authorize this Company or its agent to investigate and/or verify all information in this application, including contacting all persons, schools, current employer (if applicable), previous employers and other individuals or entities named herin (and those named on accompanying resume, if any). I hereby authorize my former employers and other third parties named on this application to release information pertaining to my work record, habits and performances. In doing so, I hereby release them and the Company and its agents from all liability which may flow from the release of such information.

I also understand and agree that no representative of the Company has any authority to enter into any agreement for employment for any specified period of time, or to make any agreement contrary to the foregoing, unless it is in writing and signed by an authorized company representative.

DATE_____SIGNATURE _____

INTERVIEWED BY_____DATE_____

APPLICATION FOR EMPLOYMENT Pre-Employment Questionnaire
Equal Opportunity Employer

Personal Information	Date	2-15-2008

NAME (Last Name First) Nancy Claxton	Social Security No. 500-02-5421

Last name first ←

Present Address 534 Midland Blvd.	City Memphis	State Tenn	Zip Code 59300

Previous Address Zip Code	City	State

Be Specific

Phone Number (Home) (810) 734-9488	Phone Number (Cell) (810) 555-9888	Referred By

Position/Employment Desired Desired Any	Date You Can Start Need time for doctor appointment	Salary

Are You Employed? __X__Yes ____No
If yes, may we inquire of your present employer? ____Yes ____No

Have you ever applied to this company before? ____Yes __X__ No
If yes, where?   When?

All people need time for appointments.

NAME AND LOCATION OF SCHOOL	YEARS ATTENDED
High School East Lake High School	4
College	
Trade, Business, or Correspondence School	

Did you graduate? →

SUBJECTS OF SPECIAL STUDY/RESEARCH

CERTIFICATIONS

US MILITARY   RANK

SPECIAL INTERESTS

FORMER EMPLOYERS (List last four, starting with the most recent first.)

DATE/MONTH/ YEAR	NAME & ADDRESS OF EMPLOYER	POSITION	SALARY	REASON FOR LEAVING
11/1999– 2/2002	AMD Hospital	CNA		Workers' Comp injury
08/1994—6/1995	Beech Industries	Quality Control	$6.85	Left to take care of children
3/1994—5/1994	McDonalds			Fired

Red Flag words— Beware of discrimination

Use positive terms

SPECIAL QUALIFICATIONS (PLEASE LIST)

_____

_____

ARE YOU AUTHORIZED TO WORK IN THE UNITED STATES?   YES   NO

(*NOTE: If you are hired, you wil be required to submit pro* ~~~~ United States.*)

> Only apply for jobs that you know you can do

CAN YOU PERFORM THE JOB WITH OR WITHOUT REASONABLE
ACCOMMODATIONS? _____YES _____X_____NO (Can't do any lifting.)

HAVE YOU EVER BEEN CONVICTED OF A FELONY? _____YES _____X_____NO
(*NOTE: If yes, please explain*)

REFERENCES: Give below the names of three persons not related to you, whom you
have known at least one year. (Would you hire this person?)

NAME	ADDRESS	TELEPHONE NUMBER	BUSINESS	YEARS KNOWN
1. Jill Thompson			Retired	16
2. Bob Claxton	3549 Drew St.	(810) 734-9488	Carpenter	Whole Life
3. Mary Briggs	Lee County Social Services	(810) 321-9087	Caseworker	4

> Looks like a relative of yours

> Is this your caseworker?

> ► Be sure to complete application with full contact information.
>
> ► Be sure to apply for a *specific* position.
>
> ► Use positive terms to describe your "reason for leaving."
>
> ► Apply only for positions that you can do.
>
> ► You can discuss accommodations during interview or after they have offered you the job.
>
> ► Make sure your references are appropriate people, *not* relatives or caseworkers.

Tips On Completing an Application for Employment

Many people have difficulty determining what to write for **"Reason for Leaving"** on the job application:

> Be honest, but be positive. If you write that you have been fired, lost a job due to an injury, or that you left for medical reasons, it gives a negative impression.

Use positive terms; here are some suggestions:

- ▶ Lay-off
- ▶ Career change
- ▶ More suitable position
- ▶ More money
- ▶ Better job
- ▶ Relocation
- ▶ Reorganization

It is **not lying** when presenting yourself more positively.

If you were a carpenter and injured your elbow, and it is painful for you to use a hammer, **a better job would be any job that did not provoke pain on a regular basis**.

> **Because you want to be honest, you will be tempted to write on your application everything about yourself. Please do not.**

Remember, it is illegal for employers to ask you about illnesses or disabilities. If you tell all, you may not get a chance to return to work.

It is human nature to discriminate. Look, for instance, at this example:

You have two friends who both want to borrow your new car:

▶ One of your friends had been in an automobile accident – it was not his fault, but he was hurt and the car needed a lot of repairs.

▶ Your other friend had a clean driving record.

To whom would you lend the car?

A person would be less likely to lend the car to someone who had an accident. This could be called discrimination since it was not the other friend's fault and was just bad luck. Nonetheless, real concerns arise when insurance and property are involved.

This is very similar to how employers choose prospective employees. Although it may seem unfair, the information will affect how a employer makes employment choices.

> **The ADA is designed to limit discrimination by making it illegal for employers to ask applicants disability related questions.**

If you volunteer information that is illegal for employers to ask, it provides employers with information that will be considered in the hiring decision, and you may influence the employer **not** to hire you.

By focusing on your qualifications, and by **not** disclosing unnecessary details about your injury or condition, you will be on an even playing field with other applicants. The prospective employer will be **less likely** to have concerns that will go against hiring you.

How do I address the problem of gaps in employment on a job application?

If you have not worked in paid employment for over a year, then you may want to write on the application what you have been doing.

Employers tend to disregard applications without recent activity.

Most people have been doing something while they are unemployed. Perhaps you have been volunteering, caring for parents, incarcerated, or caring for children.

Perhaps you have been making ends meet by doing odd jobs or selling things in flea markets or on E-Bay.

DATE/MO./ YEAR	NAME OF EMPLOYER	DUTIES	REASON FOR LEAVING
Example: 2002-2003	Bay Hospital	Volunteered in gift shop Cared for elderly	More money
1994 - present	Self-employed	Car detailing Sold merchandise on E-bay Artist Handyman	More stable employment
1997-2002	Kenwood Prison	Dietary aide Road work	Better job
1995 - present	Smith Family	Managed household of four including transportation, budgeting, shopping, and event planning.	Career change Better hours More money

Many people have gaps in their work history. Time off to care for children, ill parents, or a return to school is not unusual. Also, it takes time to find the right job.

I am having trouble remembering my exact dates of employment.

This is common. Here are some tips for remembering:

▶ Can you remember how old you were when you started working there or finished employment?

▶ Was it fall, winter, spring, or summer?

▶ If you have children, was it before or after they were born?

▶ Was it before or after you were married?

▶ What kind of car were you driving to work?

▶ Where did you live when you worked there?

If memory fails you, then call your previous employer to get exact dates of employment. If the business is closed, use your best estimate.

I have a criminal record. Should I mention this on the application?

Laws requiring disclosure of criminal records on job applications differ in each state. In most states, if you have been convicted of a felony, and if the application asks this question, then you must disclose this information. States also have different laws regarding whether or not a juvenile felony would need to be disclosed on an application and other regulations regarding expunged criminal records and misdemeanors.

Certain types of positions may not be appropriate in light of a criminal history. If you have been convicted of theft, then it may not be appropriate to apply for a locksmith position. With a history of multiple DUI convictions, a driving career may be out of the question.

A history of drug abuse will probably preclude you from working in a pharmacy and will have to be disclosed if you are applying for a nursing, physician, or other health care position.

The job I would like requires bonding. Can I get bonded if I have a criminal background?

Any "at risk" person, including ex-offenders, ex-addicts, welfare recipients, persons with poor credit, young people lacking a work history, individuals dishonorably discharged from the military, and any other person unable to secure employment without bonding is eligible for bonding through the Federal Bonding Program.

To locate the approved Federal Bonding office nearest you, call **1-877-872-5627**. This national jobs and training referral service can also direct you to local agencies for other employment-related services. You can also visit **www.bonds4jobs.com**.

Checking References

There are two types of references:

☑ Work References
☑ Personal References

A **work reference** is provided by a former employer you have listed under **work history.** Listing that former employer means that your prospective new employer may call or write to verify your employment and employment dates (see page 179).

Example:

FORMER EMPLOYERS (List below your last four employers, starting with the most recent.)

DATE/MONTH/ YEAR	NAME & ADDRESS OF EMPLOYER	SALARY	REASON FOR LEAVING

Personal References

Personal references are those listed in the reference section of an application.

Example:

References

List the name of three persons not related to you, whom you have known at least one year

NAME	ADDRESS	TEL.NO.	BUSINESS	YEARS KNOWN
1.				
2.				
3.				

A **personal reference** is a person that you have chosen to vouch for your integrity, work performance, ability to get along with others, honesty, values, dependability, character, and any other attributes the employer may explore to determine your employability with the company.

A personal reference is generally one of the following:

- ▶ Personal friends
- ▶ Volunteer friends
- ▶ Clergy
- ▶ Neighbors
- ▶ Previous co-workers
- ▶ Supervisor

I do not have many friends. May I list relatives?

Most companies do not accept references from relatives. It is acceptable to list people who live in another city which may be relevant if you have recently moved.

A prospective employer may ask your personal references any questions without restrictions. Be sure to contact your personal references before listing them on your application.

Prep your references

☑   Ask them if they would mind being a reference.

☑   Let them know what type of job you are pursuing.

☑   Update them on your medical progress and why this position would be a good fit for you.

This will help your personal references get a clearer picture of your abilities and give them a chance to think about what they would say.

Your references may also be able to provide you with valuable feedback as well as moral support.

> You never know,
>
> your reference may have knowledge
>
> of a job opening that would be just perfect for you.

Work References

Concerns about what a previous employer will say during a reference check is one of many job hunters' greatest fears.

To avoid possible charges of libel or discrimination under the Americans with Disabilities Act, many prior employers choose to disclose limited information to your prospective employer:

▶ Dates of Employment

▶ Whether or not the person is eligible for rehire

Many companies now have a 900 number handling all their reference checks. It costs money to check your references and most previous employers will release only dates of employment and job titles.

Regardless of Possible Legal Complications:

Some employers, especially smaller companies, will disclose more than dates and job titles. Be sure **not** to list such employers as references if you are afraid of a bad reference.

It may be worthwhile to have a friend or counselor call or write your references posing as a prospective employer.

By doing this, you will have a better idea how your previous employer may handle a reference check.

Sometimes a previous employer will provide a poor reference **outside of recommended legal guidelines**.

Unless you are willing to invest time and money in a legal battle, another option to consider is:

> # Name a particular person in the company as the reference contact on your application.

▶ Choose someone with whom you have had a favorable work relationship.

▶ Pick a person who knows your work and who is able to give the prospective employer a favorable impression.

Suitable work references:

> ▶ A Supervisor
>
> ▶ Human Resources Director
>
> ▶ Co-worker

Call the people you would like to list as work references and let them know your current status:

Update them about changes that may have occurred in your health, outlook, or circumstances. Let them know what type of work you are pursuing. This will prepare them if they are called for a reference check.

> ## Be sure to thank them for their assistance.

> Obtaining a clearer picture of what your references will say may alleviate some of the anxiety that often accompanies a termination of employment.

What if one of my references is unwilling to speak with a prospective employer and instead refers them to the company head or human resources department?

Many companies have a policy prohibiting managers or co-workers from giving out work references.

This policy is usually implemented because the company is afraid people may be disclosing information that is in conflict with the legal guidelines limiting what a previous employer can say to a prospective employer, thus exposing the company to a possible lawsuit.

TO DO LIST:

☑ Obtain a **written letter of personal reference** (NOT on company letterhead) from a supervisor or co-worker and attach it to the job application or resume. Bring to the interview **copies of positive job evaluations** or other documentation from previous employers that supports your work abilities and work ethics.

☑ Make a **portfolio of your work** for the prospective employer's review.

☑ Get a **letter of reference** from someone from *another* company (or from a customer) you worked with as part of your previous employment.

Another option is to send a written reference request to your previous employers. Enclose a stamped, self-addressed envelope for their convenience.

Sample letter:

July 30, 2008

To Whom It May Concern:

We are considering (your name, social security number) for employment and are checking her references. Thank you very much for your assistance.

1. Did (your name) work for your company? If so please note the dates of employment.

2. Is Ms./Mr. (last name) eligible for rehire? If not, why not.

3. Comments?

Sincerely,

Joe Trimball,
President

I authorize the release of this information to (person who is checking references for you).

_____
Signature   Date

What If I Get a Bad Reference?

If a previous employer stated that you would be ineligible for re-hire due to an injury or illness, it is <u>not necessary or recommended</u> to disclose details about your physical condition or your reason for termination in the interview.

Sample interview responses to the question: *"Why did you leave your last job?"*

► I am looking for a position that is more intellectually challenging.

► The type of job I worked in was very heavy. I would be better suited to a job that is not as strenuous.

► I am looking to work in a position that does not require frequent or constant _____ (standing, climbing, bending, typing, lifting, etc.).

► The position no longer fit my needs.

► It was by mutual agreement. I was having difficulty with the physical aspects of the job.

► I went back to school so that I could work in a different and more suitable field.

► I took some time off to re-evaluate/explore my career goals. It seems like your company is a good match for me.

► I had a situation that required me to take some time off. The situation has been resolved and I am ready to get back to work.

Now, you can fill out this application for employment.

APPLICATION FOR EMPLOYMENT
Employment Options, Inc.
1234 Anywhere Street, FL 33000

EMPLOYMENT INFORMATION

Last Name	First	Middle	Date

Street Address _____ | Home Phone (   )

City _____ County _____ | Business Phone (   )

State _____ Zip Code _____

Have you ever applied for employment with us? ____ Yes ____ No

If yes: Month and Year ____ Location _____

Position Desired _____	What days can you work (please circle) S M T W T F S	Social Security Number _____-_____-_____

Are you available full-time? _____ Part-time? _____ | Pay Expected

What hours can you work? _____ | _____

Will you work overtime? _____ Yes _____ No   When will you be available? _____

Have you ever been employed by this company?   _____ Yes _____ No

If yes, list date and location _____

_____

How were you referred to Employment Options, Inc.?

_____

_____

If your position requires the operation of vehicles, transporting of consumers, or use of personal vehicle for employment purposes, complete section relative to vehicle operation. Your driving record will be checked with the Department of Motor Vehicles.

Drivers License No. _____ State _____ Class _____

Expiration Date _____

Within the last 36 months, have you had any auto accidents or moving violations? _____ Yes _____ No: If yes, list date(s) of ALL accidents or violations, circumstances of each (including city and state) and who was at fault (to whom citation was issued): _____

_____

Are you 18 years of age or older? _____ Yes _____No

If NO, can you provide required proof of eligibility to work? _____ Yes _____No

Are you prevented from lawfully becoming employed in this country because of visa or immigration status? _____ Yes _____No

PROOF OF CITIZENSHIP OR IMMIGRATION STATUS

WILL BE REQUIRED FOR EMPLOYMENT

Have you been convicted of a felony in the last seven years? (A conviction record will not necessarily eliminate your candidacy for employment.) _____ Yes _____No

If you answered "Yes", Please explain fully, including the nature of the offense(s), and the date(s) of the offense(s), conviction(s).

_____

_____

Can you perform the essential functions of the position for which you have applied with or without reasonable accommodations? _____ Yes _____No

If No, what accommodations will you need? _____

_____

EDUCATION

School	Name & Location of School	Dates of Attendance	Course of Study	Number Of Years Completed	Did you Graduate?	Degree or Diploma
College						
High School						
Elemen-tary						
Other						
Other						

SKILLS: INDICATE SKILLS IN WHICH YOU HAVE HAD SPECIAL TRAINING.
(Please check where applicable)

☐ Typing/WPM _____   ☐ Calculator   ☐ Ten Key

☐ Computer Skills (Indicate type of software & hardware)

_____

☐ Foreign Languages _____   ☐ Speak ☐ Read ☐ Write

☐ Cash Register   ☐ PBX/Switchboard

☐ Forklift   ☐ Tractor/Trailer   ☐ Straight Truck   ☐ Other _____

Summarize special skills and/or qualifications acquired through employment and/or education or other experience.

_____

_____

_____

_____

PROFESSIONAL REFERENCES:

Please provide two references of people who have known you for two years or more whom we may contact.

Name_____

Address_____

Telephone_____   Years Known_____

Name_____

Address_____

Telephone_____   Years Known_____

EMPLOYMENT HISTORY

Company Name	Telephone ( )
Full Address	From To
Immediate Supervisor/Title	Starting Pay _____ Ending Pay _____
Your job title and description of your work	Reason for leaving __Voluntary__Layoff__Discharge Explain

Company Name	Telephone ( )
Full Address	From To
Immediate Supervisor/Title	Starting Pay _____ Ending Pay _____
Your job title and description of your work	Reason for leaving __Voluntary__Layoff__Discharge Explain

Company Name	Telephone ( )
Full Address	From To
Immediate Supervisor/Title	Starting Pay _____ Ending Pay _____
Your job title and description of your work	Reason for leaving __Voluntary__Layoff__Discharge Explain

Company Name	Telephone ( )
Full Address	From To
Immediate Supervisor/Title	Starting Pay _____ Ending Pay _____
Your job title and description of your work	Reason for leaving __Voluntary__Layoff__Discharge Explain

Please explain any gaps in your employment history._____

_____

Have you ever been employed under a different name? ____ Yes ____ No

List Names _____ _____

We may contact the employers listed above unless you indicate those you do not want us to contact. List those employers here. Please include your reason.

_____ _____

I hereby certify that the answers and statements in this application are true and complete, I understand that any misrepresentation or omission of facts in this application may disqualify me from further consideration for employment, and, if employed, will subject me to dismissal at any time without previous notice.

I authorize Employment Options, Inc. or agent of Employment Options, Inc. to investigate my references, and that I may be subject to a criminal background check by local, state and/or federal law enforcement agencies.

I understand that an offer of employment with Employment Options, Inc. is contingent upon my taking and passing a test for illegal drugs and favorable pre-employment background investigation results.

Employment Options Inc. is an equal opportunity employer. We adhere to a policy of making employment decisions without regard to race, color, age, sex, religion, national origin, sexual orientation, marital status, veteran, handicap or disabled status.

_____   _____
Signature   Date

NOTICE: This application will remain active for ninety (90) days. Any applicant wishing to be considered for employment beyond ninety (90) days must reapply.

(TO BE COMPLETED BY HIRING AUTHORITY)

Date of Hire _____	Employee Number _____	Time Card No. _____
Job Title _____	Hourly Rate of Pay _____	Charge Code _____
Department _____	Location _____	Supervisor_____

☐ **PART-TIME**   ☐ **FULL-TIME**   ☐ **TEMPORARY**

_____
Signature and Title of Hiring Authority
FORM #611 REV 11/97

Make a copy of your corrected application and bring it with you when you job search. It is easier to copy your information onto their application instead of trying to remember it all.

Resumes & Cover Letters

A resume is your opportunity to highlight your skills, goals, and experience. Step by step, you will learn how to write a resume that gets results.

Many of the resume samples included in this chapter target specific challenges. You will learn what to present and why.

Be sure to have someone look at your resume for spelling and other errors before you send it out!

Mistakes are easy to miss and leave a very poor impression with the prospective employer.

A good resume can open doors.

Do I Need A Resume?

> **The primary purpose of a resume is to obtain an interview.**

If you are able to find employers interested in interviewing you without a resume, then you may not need a resume.

▶ How is a resume different from an application?

A resume is like taking a picture of yourself. It presents an image of your skills, abilities, interests, and experience. A resume can highlight skills or interests that you would like to use more in your next position.

An application asks for specific information. Generally, an application asks for your previous employment history, education, and references. An application leaves little room to talk about your interests, goals, or transferable skills.

> **If you are changing careers, it is helpful to have a resume so that you can emphasize those skills and abilities you would use in a new occupation.**

▶ What is a transferable skill?

A transferable skill is a technical term that describes activities you have performed in your past jobs that will also be used in a new job.

▶ How do I know if my resume is any good?

Resumes are a bit like taste buds. You may like a resume and the person next to you may think it needs revising.

A Good Resume Gets Results!

The average **human resource director** will spend about **twenty seconds** reading a resume. Thus, a one-page resume summing up your work experience and skills is preferable.

If your work history is quite involved and you are applying for a higher level position such as CEO, a longer resume or *curriculum vitae* may be more appropriate.

If you are applying for a job that requests a scannable resume, that means your resume will be read by a computer that will be looking to identify buzz words or words specific to your profession (such as a CPA or MCP).

▶ How do I know if I need a scannable resume?

Usually employers will indicate if they are looking for a *scannable* resume. Guidelines for scannable resumes are a little different:

Use of italics, underlining, shadows, bullets, and boxes are difficult for the computer to read and are not recommended

Use of common fonts, such as Times New Roman and Courier, is recommended

Avoid using two-column formats and graphics

▶ I am not sure how to get started on a resume.

It may help you to look at different resume books to choose the style you like best.

▶ Should I go to a professional resume writer to write my resume?

It can be helpful to hire a professional resume writer or to work with a vocational or career counselor.

Pick someone who is familiar with the job market, who can objectively describe your skills, and who can help you develop an objective.

You can also look at the sample resumes presented on the following pages and use one as a model for building your own resume.

In the following pages, discover how different resumes achieve different goals.

Sample Functional Resume A functional resume that works well for persons changing careers:

Bill Thompson
9100 Main Street.
St. Petersburg, Florida 33712
(727) 956-0199

OBJECTIVE: *Technical- electrical and Customer Service*

PROFILE: Well rounded, courteous, creative, and flexible individual

SUMMARY OF QUALIFICATIONS:
> Hands-on experience with AC/DC circuiting, hydraulics, pneumatics, magnetics
> Experience with step-up and step-down transformers and familiar with Y+ and Delta
> Electrical wiring up to box - including 240 x 480 volt electric and 3 phase electric and controls
> A/C experience with thermostats, refrigeration, controls, and solenoids
> Computer literate: Windows; Typing, 30 wpm
> Team player - good at interpersonal skills

EDUCATION:
> **St. Petersburg Tech Institute**, St. Petersburg, Florida, 3.0 GPA
>> Certified as Industrial Electrician
>> VICA member, Vocational Industrial Clubs of America
>> Air Conditioning and Heating
> *Accomplishments: Rotary scholarship recipient*
> **Public Works Academy**, St. Petersburg, Florida

WORK HISTORY:
> **Minute Press,** St. Petersburg, Florida, 4 years
>> <u>Machine Press Operator</u>
>>> Assembly line work collecting and stacking phone books

> **Town and Country Yacht Club,** St. Petersburg, Florida
>> <u>Maintenance/Housekeeping</u> 1 year
>>> Maintained facilities - setting up and breaking down banquets

> **Suncoast Dome,** St. Petersburg, Florida
>> <u>Commissary Manager</u> 2 years
>>> Working supervisor of seven people
>>> Responsible for scheduling, distribution, manifesting, stocking, janitorial, and maintenance

> **American Utilities**, Clearwater, Fl
> <u>Electrician helper</u> 2 years

HOBBIES: Surfing the Internet and cooking

Reviewing Bill's Resume

Bill Thompson had been working in a heavy job as a press operator and needed to get into something lighter.

His education and skills were listed first since they were his strongest selling points.

His objective stressed his customer service and technical background with the hopes that he would be considered for a position in customer service, as a industrial electrician or light maintenance worker.

> **Always put your strongest points first!**

**Below are the answers to some of the questions
you may have about Bill's resume:**

Why did he leave out the dates of his education?

Putting in dates of education tips off an employer as to the age of the applicant. Also, since Bill had some gaps in his recent employment history, putting his education first took the focus off those gaps.

The advantage of a resume is that it presents an applicant's positive qualities in a way that makes a prospective employer interested in interviewing the applicant.

Why did he put the dates as number of years instead of specifying the exact years that he worked?

Bill worked quite a number of jobs between the ones listed on the resume. The jobs that he chose to list on the resume were the ones that he felt were the most relevant to the position.

Bill was offered two positions with this resume:

The first offer was as a telephonic customer service representative for a major telephone company.

The second was as an assistant maintenance supervisor.

MARY LINCOLN

2052 Marietta Road
St Petersburg, Florida 33713
(727) 321-0273

OBJECTIVE: COSMETOLOGY INSTRUCTOR

PROFILE: Professional, Stable, Self-motivated, and Productive individual

SUMMARY OF QUALIFICATIONS:

Licensed cosmetologist
Certified in Joe Blasco make-up
Seasoned manager
Excellent interpersonal skills

WORK HISTORY:

1995 - 2000   **Fashion Haircuts -** St. Petersburg, Florida
<u>Salon Manager</u>
Supervised up to 10 person staff - scheduling, hiring and firing
Organized and led monthly meeting

Accomplishments: Sixth Highest in Sales in Nation
Won Color Competition

1993 - 1995   **Sandy Morris Glamour Studio**, St. Petersburg, Florida
<u>Make up artist; Stylist</u>

1990 - 1993   **Fantastic Sams**, St. Petersburg, Florida
<u>Hair stylist</u>

1986 - 1988   **Ready Dispatch,** St. Petersburg, Florida
<u>Field Representative</u>
Evaluated and trained drivers

PROFESSIONAL LICENSES: Cosmetology - Manhattan Beauty School, Tampa, Florida, **Refresher courses in Cosmetology**
CPR & First Aid -Manatee Community College, Venice, FL

COMMUNITY INVOLVEMENT: Broadway Productions, St. Petersburg, FL
Make-up and casting

HOBBIES: Movies, cooking, and computers

(References available upon request)

After a long military career, Walter was looking for employment in the civilian world. He emphasized his flexibility and tasks in human resources, changing vocabulary as necessary to match civilian jobs.

WALTER SIMMONS
10692 Turkey Creek Drive
Arlington, VA
(680) 725-9932

OBJECTIVE: HUMAN RESOURCE ASSISTANT

PROFILE: A flexible, hard-working, and organized human resource professional with over 15 years of human resource experience

SUMMARY OF QUALIFICATIONS:
Computer literate, including Word, Windows, & Lotus 1,2,3
Excellent interpersonal skills
Efficient and effective coordinator
Skilled at conflict resolution
Adept with paperwork and regulations

WORK EXPERIENCE: 1985 -2004
United States Army, Washington, D.C.
Human Resource Specialist, SHAPE
Staff recruiting, new employee orientations and training
Coordination of temporary and freelance staff
Analyzed personnel for job assignments
Supervised personnel in customer service

Personnel Specialist, Washington, D.C
Security manager for personnel clearances
Assisted a variety of personnel functions, including screening resumes, coordinating interviews, processing orders, and correspondence

Personnel Specialist, Karlsruhe & Pirmasens, Germany
Supervised all personnel functions: processing assignments, leaves, and customer service for two military communities over 6,000 in strength
Accomplishments: Streamlined 'Port of Call" procedures for travel reservations resulting in $100,000-200,0000 annual savings

EDUCATION: University of West Virginia
Management, Accounting, and general studies coursework

MILITARY: UNITED STATES ARMY: Rank E-5, Honorable Discharge

VOLUNTEER ACTIVITIES: Youth basketball and baseball coach

Jerry's background was in finance, but he was open to other types of sales and management positions. He emphasized his education and described his skills as an account executive that were relevant to sales and management. He omitted his professional licenses in the finance industry so as not to draw attention to his highly-specialized field.

JERRY CHARTS
240 East 59th St.
New York City, NY 69002
(567) 355-9999

OBJECTIVE: Sales & Management

PROFILE: A seasoned professional desiring a career change to a position that will benefit from my ability to analyze and manage, work independently and as part of a team, and to promote and close sales.

SUMMARY OF QUALIFICATIONS:
Strong sales and customer service background
Excellent written, verbal, and telephonic communication skills
Skilled at relationship building and loyalty sales
Able to assess company performance and growth projections
Financial management and administration
Computer literate: Internet, Microsoft Office

EDUCATION:
University of Florida, Gainesville, Florida
Bachelor of Arts in Economics: Business Management and Marketing

MILITARY: United States Army: Rank E-4, Honorable Discharge

WORK HISTORY:

1989 - Present   **Smith Barney**, New York City
Associate Vice President
Managed multi-million dollar accounts as well as smaller accounts
Developed appropriate financial plan and goals helping select investments including stocks, bonds, mutual funds, unit trusts, insurance, tax-exempt investments, retirement and trust services, credit products and services.

1982 - 1989   **Northwest Mutual,** Chicago, IL
Account Executive
Managed all different volumes of accounts
Financial planning including investments in stocks, bonds, mutual funds, trusts, insurance, tax exempt investments, and retirement planning.

COMMUNITY INVOLVEMENT: March of Dimes Volunteer Coordinator

As Sam did not have much real world experience in accounting, he listed the skills that he had acquired in school.

Sam Patel - CPA
352 Magnolia Dr
Atlanta, GA 33684-5114

E-mail: Patel983@aol.com   Tel/Fax: (404) 923-3211   Cell: (404) 390-6053

OBJECTIVE: **To secure an entry-level professional accounting position with a growing company.**

PROFILE: A hard-working, willing-to-learn and detail-oriented accounting graduate with computer and customer service skills. CPA certified.

SUMMARY OF SKILLS:
Computer savvy: Excel, Word, Access, PowerPoint, Peachtree, Quickbooks, SQL, JavaScript, ASP, Web page design, Java.
7800 Keypunch/hour.
GAAP accounting, Federal income taxation, Auditing, Cost Accounting
Grade A in Public Speaking classes and Honors Thesis
Excellent written and verbal communication skills

EDUCATION: University of Georgia, GA   32981
Masters of Accountancy, graduated 12/2003   **GPA: 3.56**

University of Georgia, GA   32981
Bachelors of Science in Accounting, graduated 12/2000   **GPA: 3.30**

AWARDS: Registration Fee and Book Scholarship
Member of the University-wide Honors Program
Member of the National Golden Key Honors Program

WORK BACKGROUND:
5/2006 - 5/2008   **University of Georgia**
Computer Lab Assistant
► Learned software features and became proficient in all computer software implemented in the lab
► Assisted students with questions concerning software and programs
► Maintained computer lab equipment: computers, printers, and software
► Enforced laboratory policies and procedures

HOBBIES: Working out, doing research, writing, reading, and gardening.

(References available upon request)

Jane was interested in getting hired by a company that would provide her with the opportunity to work in a foreign country. She targeted her resume to emphasize her understanding of other cultures and her versatility.

JANE BASSET
7490 Southside Blvd.
Jacksonville, Florida 32256
(850) 983-9855
e-mail: JBASSET@mindspring.com

PROFILE: Fast-learner, new graduate seeking career opportunities, seeking employment with a multi-national company

EDUCATION: UNIVERSITY OF FLORIDA, Gainesville, Florida
• BA in International Relations: **3.79 GPA,** *magna cum laude*
• Minor: Psychology

COMPUTER SKILLS:
• Software: Word, Word Perfect, Excel, PowerPoint, Internet
• 40+ WPM

SKILLS TO NOTE:
  • Fluent in French
  • Excellent communication and presentation skills
  • Comfortable with responsibility and leadership
  • Great telephone skills
  • Interests in Photography and Theatre
  • Work experience in Retail, Customer Service, Sales, and Bookkeeping

CLASSES TAKEN:
• Epidemiology, Economic Geography, Cross-Cultural Methodologies, Biology I & II, Psychobiology, People and Cultures of the World, Contemporary Economic Issues, International Law and Organization, French (Intermediate and Advanced), many Psychology courses

COMMUNITY ACTIVITIES:
  Treasurer of Sawmill Slough Environmental Club, Jan. 2003-current
  Volunteer at Bayfront Hospital as Student Ambassador (Pediatrics unit)

(Work experience and references available upon request)

Tracy has freelanced for various vocational rehabilitation companies for years. Although she had worked in other jobs, her resume referred only to work that was relevant to the position for which she was applying. Rather than listing all of the companies where she contracted work, she grouped them together, adding cohesiveness to her employment history.

Tracy Hatter

28 Morning Glory Ave.
Tampa, FL 33899
Phone: (813) 683-4300

thatter@verizon.net

Objective: *Career Development Counselor*

QUALIFICATIONS:
    Fifteen years of experience assisting individuals in securing employment commensurate with their vocational goals, interests, and economic needs. Achieving these goals requires:
    Evaluating educational or training requirements of target employment;
    Researching and **identifying** jobs within the community;
    Marketing prospective employees to business and industry in the community through direct contact and telephone surveys;
    Editing and **reviewing** of resumes, cover letters and other materials required for application to a specific position; and
    Coaching applicants in **networking** skills and **interviewing** skills.

EDUCATION
1962-1965   University of Wisconsin-Milwaukee, WI
1971-1973   Long Beach City College, Long Beach, CA
1973-1978   University of New Mexico, Albuquerque, NM, BA Degree, 1978

RELATED EMPLOYMENT HISTORY
1991-2002, Freelance Job Development and Placement Specialist for local Vocational Rehabilitation Companies:
    Solved complex reemployment issues for vocational rehabilitation clients. **Identified** job openings by canvassing industries and businesses in the targeted areas.

1989-1991, Vocational Rehabilitation Consultant, Carriers Rehabilitation:
    Assessed client's level of needs for services. **Evaluated** clients for special vocational testing and retraining needs. **Coached** individual job-seeking skills and interview techniques. **Prepared** applications and resumes for clients. **Counseled** clients on employment issues and monitored progress after placement to identify any workplace issues. **Marketed** business services with insurance companies and state agencies. **Developed** network of employers with reoccurring labor needs.

Sales Charles was ready for new challenges. Although he enjoyed his work, it involved quite a bit of traveling as his territory covered the whole Northeast. Charles was interested in exploring the job market to find a job that did not require him to be away so much.

CHARLES POWELL
4501 Tanner Blvd.
Birmingham, Alabama

Ph: (930) 896-4055   e-mail: cpowell2259@hotmail.com

OBJECTIVE: ACCOUNT EXECUTIVE OR SALES MANAGEMENT POSITION
with a quality company where my sales, relationship building, and professional knowledge can contribute to growth and profitability

PROFILE: Motivated and experienced high-end technical sales

SUMMARY OF QUALIFICATIONS:

Self directed and disciplined - excellent time management skills

Goal driven - enjoys challenge and growth

Able to recognize and analyze profitable business

Proven ability to lead a team, develop goals, and increase/close sales

Effective communicator - ability to relate to decision makers at all levels

PROFESSIONAL EXPERIENCE:

PRIME ELECTRONICS, New York, NY, Fortune 500 Company
1993 - Present: Worldwide distributor of electronic products, including semiconductors, passives, electromechanical devices, interconnect and industrial computer products

Account Executive - Territory Manager for Northeastern States

Solicited new accounts, manage and develop existing accounts for electronic semiconductor product needs

Interfaced with engineers, purchasing, sales & marketing, CEOs and CFOs to identify company needs

Recommended appropriate products and technology, assisted with company's marketing and sales strategies, and established and qualified lines of credit

Accomplishments: #1 Salesperson in 1998 & 1999
Consistently hit or exceeded sales quotas
Shipped from $500k - $750k monthly

WRIGHT CORPORATION, Birmingham, Alabama
1990 - 1993: Manufacturer of Electronic Enclosures and Housing
Account Executive/ Inside Sales Representative

Conducted showroom presentations and product training seminars

Trained staff on product knowledge, customer service, and administrative duties

Accomplishments: Managed Key, House, and Distributor Accounts that generated over $3.5 million in revenue in 1992 from $2.2 million in 1991

EDUCATION: UNIVERSITY OF NORTH CAROLINA AT GREENSBORO

Tammy was hoping to get a job in a smaller clinic. To show that she was flexible and well-rounded, she made sure to list some of the duties she had performed as a medical assistant.

TAMMY NORRIS

18-20TH St. North
Raleigh, NC 98006
Home Phone 973-682-0448

Q U A L I F I C A T I O N S

Take and process x-rays
Cat scans
Contrast media injections
Patient vitals
Assist doctors with minor surgery and casting
Assist nurses with oncology patients
Ordered medical and office supplies
Responsible for back office yearly inspections
Responsible for emergency equipment
Front office duties and insurance referrals

W O R K   H I S T O R Y

Radiologic Technologist, Memorial Regional Hospital
11/97-8/00   Raleigh, NC

Radiologic Technologist, Regional Medical Center
9/98-9/99   Peoria, IL

Medical Assistant, John Simmons M.D.
5/97-10/97   Peoria, IL

Radiologic Tech/Medical Assistant, Emory Hospital
2/92-10/96   Atlanta, GA

E D U C A T I O N

ARRT, Cooper Hospital, NJ
Peoria Advanced Imaging Institute, Accelerated Course 1993

L I C E N S E S   &   C E R T I F I C A T E S

ARRT

Skills-based Resume

Although Janet had worked in the computer field for many years, both at the telephone company and in her own business, in light of rapidly advancing technology, many of the programs that she had used in those positions were outdated. She remained up-to-date on software through self-study and continuing education. By using a skill based resume, we were able to highlight her multiple skills.

JANET SUMMERS
1920 Oak Drive, Green Bay, WI 51788
(920) 873-0941
e:mail: jsummers@webmastersinc.com   www: webmastersinc.com

Objective: A challenging and rewarding position in interactive multimedia, computer graphics or videography

Profile: A visually-oriented and technically savvy multimedia specialist

Summary of Qualifications:

Operating Systems: MS Windows 9.x, NT, XP, MacIntosh, Linux RedHat, SuSe and X-Windows, Programming in HTML, DHTML, VRML, XML, CGI, PEARL, JAVA and many others.

Software Applications: Photo retouch, paint, animation, 3D rendering, virtual reality and web-graphic applications. Audio and video digitizing, mixing, editing, effects and live Internet streaming:

Photo and Paint	Animation, Interactive Multimedia & 3D Rendering	
Adobe Photo Shop, Illustrator	Adobe GoLive,	Live Motion
Corel Draw, Designer	* Macromedia MX	Renderman
Image Forge Pro	Animagic (.gif anims)	Mental Ray
Paint Shop Pro	Swish (flash anims)	Lightwave
	3D Flash Animator	Softimage
Audio Mixing and Effects	PowerPoint	Scala
Sound Forge		Maya
RealAudio	**Virtual Reality**	
Cool Edit	JSP (java server pages)	
ProTools	VRML Beans	

* Macromedia MX includes: Dreamweaver, Flash, Fireworks, and Director Shockwave Studio

Military: Air Force ROTC - Second Lieutenant, instrument flight rated pilot

Education:

University of Wisconsin, **Bachelor of Science: Computer Science**

Wisconsin College of Art and Design, **Bachelor of Fine Arts**: photography, videography, computer graphics and sculpture

Work History:

Web Masters Interactive, Green Bay, WI., 1998-present
Web site design, programming, hosting, electronic commerce, graphic design, and publishing

SBC Communications, (Northeastern Minnesota Region), 1981-1996
District Manager: Intra-office computer networking and programming divisions.

ROBERT TALLON

1124 10TH Av.
Orlando, Florida 33512
(305) 512-3536

PROFILE: Self-starter, good at decision making, quality control and reading people

SUMMARY OF QUALIFICATIONS:

> Managed all facets of hotel business with restaurant.
> Group leader
> Well-organized and a good leader

MILITARY BACKGROUND

> **Army Rank E-4**
> <u>Supply Sergeant</u>, responsible for shipping and receiving

WORK HISTORY:

> **Wig Wam Hotel,** Lake Ontario, NY, 15 years
> <u>Manager</u>
>> Operated hotel with 13 sleeping rooms
>> Profitably ran restaurant seating 145 persons
>> Managed up to 35 people
>> Hired, trained, scheduled employees
>> Scheduled all special events: banquets, weddings, etc.
>> Responsible for marketing, profit/loss, and purchasing

> **GTE, Allentown,** Pennsylvania, 15 years
> <u>Group Leader, Manufacturing</u>
>> Supervised 60 people on two shifts
>> Responsible for quality control and productivity
>> Skilled with machine shop operations, parts installations, tungsten reduction and apertures

Additional Work History - Asbestos abatement (with license)

HOBBIES: Internet, traveling, woodworking

Michael had been in construction before he made a career change into a seaman position. After a shoulder injury left him unable to work as a seaman, he targeted a return to work as a construction superintendent in a position that is light in nature.

MICHAEL TOMLINSON
563 Oakland Drive, Miami, Florida
Ph: (838) 224-9733

OBJECTIVE: Construction Supervisor - Construction Superintendent - Project manager - Estimator

PROFILE: Over eight years experience in all facets of construction management

SUMMARY OF QUALIFICATIONS:

Superintendent of government and commercial projects up to 15 MM

Extensive knowledge of construction materials and processes

Experienced estimator and proven sales, up to 1/4 MM

Building codes, rules, regulations, and permitting: Standard, South Florida, Marine, Government

OSHA: Basic safety and compliance standards

Team Player: Engineers, Owners, and Inspectors

Comfortable with Computers: Estimating and construction software, Word, Outlook

Bi-Lingual (Spanish)

PROFESSIONAL EXPERIENCE:

1999 - 2002   **COASTAL SHIPPING,** Miami, Florida, <u>Able Seaman</u>
Assisted in ship operations, machinery maintenance and repair
Communications and safety

1997 - 1999   **SDI,** Coconut Creek, Florida, <u>Superintendent of Construction</u>
General Construction firm—estimated, contracted and managed for projects, including remodeling, additions and new construction
Hired, fired and managed sub-contractors and employees

1993 - 1997   **INTERCOASTAL MARINE, S.A.,** Panama, <u>Marine Superintendent</u>
In charge of large-scale marine construction and diving operations
Underwater and above-water construction (piers and docks)
Accomplishments: Managed construction of a Fire Prevention Systems, which included construction of 16 monitor towers and pumphouses

1991 - 1993   **KUNKEL & WEISE,** Panama, FL, <u>Superintendent and Quality Control</u>
General construction management (refineries)
Managed crew of 20
Accomplishments: Quality Control for Panama Canal Commission and

David did not want to do over-the-road trucking as he did not want to be away for long periods. He was very specific in the objective, and we made sure that we included all the information that trucking companies normally request.

David L. Boston
9697-55th Avenue North, Seminole, Florida 33777
(727) 461-2933

OBJECTIVE: Position with stable and reputable company as a local truck driver

LICENSURES:
- Class A driver's license with Hazmat, Doubles, and Triples Endorsement
- Current DOT card

SUMMARY OF QUALIFICATIONS:
- Experienced pulling doubles, tractor-trailers, straight trucks, and cargo vans
- Dependable
- Over 10 years as a professional driver
- Safe driver
- Adept at maintaining log books and collecting payment for merchandise

MILITARY: United State Army, Rank E-4, Honorable Discharge

PROFESSIONAL EXPERIENCE:

1996- 2000   **Hairwork Co.** Largo, Florida
Driver
- Delivered merchandise in van to beauty parlors and shops statewide in Florida

1993 - 1995   **Ace Parcel Service,** Largo, Florida
Driver
- Drove straight trucks, tractor-trailers, and doubles
- Delivered parcel packages to malls throughout Pinellas County

1990 - 1993   **Tasty Foods,** Cincinnati, Ohio
Driver
- Delivered refrigerated and frozen foods in a 250-mile radius of Cincinnati
- Drove straight trucks and tractor-trailers

1988 - 1990   **Chemex Paints,** Tampa, Florida
Plant Manager
- Supervised ten workers in a manufacturing environment
- Responsible for production department, shipping and receiving
- Ordering of products and quality control

EDUCATION: G.E.D.

Mary's profile does an excellent job of describing her. In just a few words, she was able to focus on her abilities.

MARY DORROW
1616 Nantucket Court, Lexington, KY 70839
(613) 870-3556

PROFILE: *A project-oriented, persuasive and organized writer with over ten years of professional copy writing, technical writing, newspaper columns, newsletters, and advertisement copy experience*

OBJECTIVE: Strong interest in grant writing, technical writing and development of written communications material

SUMMARY OF SKILLS:
- Computer: Microsoft Word, Excel, CorelDraw, Internet, Windows XP and Vista
- 80-90 wpm
- Proficient with technical and medical terminology
- Analyzing matchprints and bluelines in pre-press stage of production
- Extremely detail-oriented
- Able to meet deadlines, work independently and with teams
- Research: Internet proficiency
- Excellent written and verbal communication skills

WORK BACKGROUND:

1994- 1999, **Curtin & Pease/ Peneco**, Dunedin, Florida, <u>Copy Editor</u>
- Production of advertising and technical material
- Proof-reading and editing of specialized medical/pharmaceutical copy
- Assisted in writing/editing of a Wellness program to be sold to HMO's
- Internet research
- Reference tracking and documentation

Accomplishments: Edited a Continuing Medical Education course aimed at specialty physicians wanting to expand their knowledge of general practice

1991- 1992, **Healthcare,** Largo, Florida, <u>Freelance Technical Writer</u>
- Researched and wrote a service manual for a blood pump
- Conferred with project engineers
- Compiled technical and reference information for repair techs

Other Work Experience includes: Secretarial work for a Virginia Legislative Commission, insurance broker, and real estate banker

EDUCATION: Christopher Newport University, Newport, Virginia (English major)

David has a personality disorder that makes it difficult for him to work with other people on a frequent basis. To his credit, he is extremely detail-oriented, which is a must in some jobs. With this resume, he was hired at a title company that processes mortgages.

DAVID WELLER
4590 Crystal Ave.

Telephone (820) 5116   Dayton, Ohio 39885   e-mail: dw5301@aol.com

OBJECTIVE: Shipping/receiving - Records Clerk- Mailroom Clerk

PROFILE: Detail-oriented, organized and efficient self-starter who thrives in work environments requiring a person to work independently and precisely.

SUMMARY OF QUALIFICATIONS:
- Computerized inventory management
- Microsoft Office 2000 - Word, Excel, Access, and PowerPoint
- Typing - 40 wpm
- Safe Florida Driver's License, Class D
- Good with numbers and proofreading

WORK EXPERIENCE:

DART   Dayton, Ohio
Staff Assistant   Jan 2006 to June 2008
- Worked in group home for the developmentally disabled offering general support, including typing case notes, filing and maintaining general paperwork
- Incorporated HIPAA requirements into program
- Light maintenance - yard work, housework, meal preparation

Autohouse Buick   Dayton, Ohio
Warehouse Worker/Delivery   August 2000 to December 2005
- Parts delivery
- Maintained inventory, received and tracked parts
- Customer service
- Filing

Target   Dayton, Ohio
Clerk/Cashier/Stocker   March 1997 to January 1998
- Handled cash register
- Customer service
- Stock and maintained stockroom
- Prepared lesson plans and daily activities

EDUCATION: University of Ohio - Bachelor's of Science
                Jackson Community College - PC Support Services

Mr. Jones had retired and later decided to return to work. So as not to draw attention to his age, he only went back fifteen years on the resume. He also made sure that he had an e-mail address, showing that he keeps up with technology.

STEVEN JONES
874- 9TH Street North
St. Louis, MO 35391

e-mail: sjone1195@ aol.com   **(461) 295-1480**

OBJECTIVE: OFFICE ADMINISTRATOR

PROFILE: **Proven manager** with strong financial, computer training, and business development experience. Loves a challenge. Comfortable with responsibility and leadership.

EDUCATION: **American University** – Washington, D.C.
Bachelor of Science in Business Management

SUMMARY OF QUALIFICATIONS
- Computer Savvy - Word, Excel, PowerPoint, Internet, Desktop Publishing, Windows
- Purchasing - 50mm annual budget
- Managed staff of up to 50 in call centers, outside sales and retail management
- Financial Accounting, Budgeting
- Training Manager
- Computer troubleshooting and repair

PROFESSIONAL EXPERIENCE:
2000 - 2003   **Mom's Handyman & Cleaning Services,** Business Set-up
- Assisted wife with company set-up and estimating

1997 - 2000   **NU Manufacturing** – Earth City, MO
Factory Representative - Estimator
- High-end customer service and sales
- Prepared bids per customer specifications
- Handled all paperwork used in procurement of permits

Accomplishment: Monitored projects from inception to completion for quality and to assure project timeliness

1988 - 1997   **MIXA, Inc.** – Washington, MO, Sales Manager
- Trained and managed new sales representatives and franchise owners in sales and all associated marketing in a specialized video advertising field.
- Wrote training manual and assisted with human resources.

Handyman

Jim is the kind of guy who would not often need a resume; he would find jobs through referrals. Once Jim left Treemont, he did not know as many people. As he has so many skills, his resumes were customized depending on the type of work he was pursuing.

JIM WALKER
520-108th Way
Santa Barbara, CA

Tel: (843) 581-8900
Email: repairforu@earthlink.com

PROFILE: Honest, dependable, self-motivated, and resourceful team player with above average sales, customer service, and mechanical ingenuity

SUMMARY OF QUALIFICATIONS: Electrical & mechanical: Troubleshooting, maintenance, manufacturing and installation. Built, sold, and serviced a wide variety of systems including:

Lawn care equipment: Mowers, edgers, chainsaws and trimmers
Restaurant and supermarket equipment: Ovens: gas and electric. Automatic wrappers. Meat room machinery: Grinders, saws and slicers
Tools: Air compressors, hydraulic pumps, battery chargers, air tools, wood working
Machine repair: Packaging, printing, folding and woodworking equipment
Computer: Repair and updating hardware and software installation
Music: Recondition and repair all string instruments and sound equipment
Sales: Retail, commercial, automobile and industrial

Skills include: Blueprint reading, pneumatics, plumbing, electrical: up 220 volts, injection mold setting, ability to work with engineers on prototypes

WORK EXPERIENCE:
1999-2000   **STILLWELL,** Santa Barbara, Ca.
      <u>Research and Development, Chemical Engineering and Manufacturing</u>
    ◊   Collaborated on experimental prototype machine that takes water and transforms it into a usable combustible gas through chemical and mechanical manipulation

1997-1998   **MATTRESS LAND,** Santa Monica, Ca.
      <u>Assistant Manager</u>
    ◊ Responsible for store sales and management

1995-1997   **BOB'S PAWN SHOP,** Treemont, Ca.
      <u>Manager, musical and equipment repair departments</u>
    ◊   Bought, sold and repaired musical instruments and equipment
    ◊   Responsible for repair work on cameras, tools, computer, engines, pneumatics, lawn care equipment and electrical instrumentation

1983-1994   **MARTIN'S SUPERMARKET,** Triton, Nebraska

Notice the emphasis here on qualifications. Beverly has so many marketable skills that the gap in recent employment goes unnoticed.

BEVERLY PALMER
1021 Meadowwood Blvd.
Phoenix, Arizona 87335
Home Phone (573) 366-3390

OBJECTIVE: Full-time <u>Customer Service Representative </u>in a day shift position with a quality company

PROFILE: Detail-oriented, responsible, motivated worker who enjoys challenging work

SUMMARY OF QUALIFICATIONS:

- High-volume call center experience
- Adept at problem-solving, researching, and resolving issues
- Sales and service
- Title work - Mortgages - Supervision
- Able to communicate with people of all levels
- Computer literate - Word, Windows, 50 wpm

WORK HISTORY:

USA Collections, Phoenix, AZ 1994-2000
<u>Assistant Supervisor</u>

- Initiated calls to individuals who were delinquent on their mortgages
- Skip tracing to locate persons
- Direct supervision of 5-6 persons
- Trained new staff on collection laws and telephone skills
- Made final decisions regarding reduced payment options for customers

The Flyer, Philadelphia, PA 1992-1994
<u>Classified ad advisor/Sales</u>

- Advised and assisted customers with ads for local newspaper
- Personalized assistance in developing effective custom advertising
- Cash and credit card processing
- Worked in commission sales with a base salary

ABX, Pittsburgh, PA 1991-1992
<u>Title Processor</u>

- Typed up title policies for homes according to specifications
- Answered phones and general office duties.

EDUCATION: Curtis High School, Staten Island, New York
High School Diploma

(References upon Request)

A C.V. (*curriculum vitae*) is often requested for public speakers, expert witnesses, board members, political and executive positions, and other high-level employment where a more detailed history of a person's professional work and community involvement is indicated.

RONALD DUBBELD
3167 Starway Street
Baker, Nevada, 59881
(605) 489-1264

Curriculum Vitae

PROFILE:

An experienced educator with expertise in employment discrimination law. Skilled in working with community organizations to maximize their efforts in working with city and state governments.

Experienced in volunteer work with agencies providing special needs to the community. Adept in working with persons from diverse cultures, backgrounds, educational levels, and varying opinions.

LICENSURES:

A.A.	History, St. Petersburg Junior College, St. Petersburg, FL
B.A.	History/Political Science, Stillman College, Tuscaloosa, AL
M.E.D.	English/Curriculum Planning, Temple University, Philadelphia, PA
J.D.	University of Florida, College of Law, Gainesville, FL

AFFILIATIONS:

KAPPA ALPHA PSI Fraternity
PHI ALPHA DELTA Legal Fraternity,
University of Florida, College of Law
LIONS CLUB, Atlantic City, NJ
BOARD OF DIRECTORS, Atlantic City Dance Theatre
MEMBER OF LEGISLATIVE DELEGATION,
Pennsylvania State House and Senate
FORMER CHAIRMAN OF BOARD OF DIRECTORS,
Atlantic City Family Center

SPECIAL EVENTS:

STUDENT MARSHAL - Dr. Martin Luther King's Funeral Cortege, Atlanta, GA, 1968

SPECIAL ENVOY - Million Man March, Washington, DC, 1992

EXCHANGE STUDENT - Political Education Seminar, George Washington University, Washington, DC, 1974

RONALD DUBBELD
3167 Starway Street
Baker, Nevada, 59881
(605) 489-1264

WORK EXPERIENCE:

LEGAL ANALYST - SENIOR INVESTIGATOR, State Attorney General of NY,
1986 -1996   Department Law and Public Safety, Buffalo, NY

Analyzed legal memoranda, investigated discriminatory complaints
based on New Jersey laws against discrimination and federal
statutes. I determined findings of probable and no cause.
Managed and supervised an office in Buffalo, NY.

CITY OF SPRINGHILL, NJ, HUMAN RELATIONS INVESTIGATOR
1984 -1985

Investigated discrimination complaints (employment and public
accommodations) in accordance with the city ordinance of Springhill
and federal statutes. (EEOC)

1981 -1982 **LEGAL COUNSEL TO STATE SENATOR CHARLES FORD,**
New Jersey

1981 **LEGISLATIVE AIDE TO STATE REPRESENTATIVE**
CHARLES FORD, New Jersey

1980 -1981 **LAW FIRM OF SMITH, PAULEY, JOHNSON & ROE**
Sanford, New Jersey. Managed law office, took depositions and assisted
in criminal trials. Performed various legal duties.

1976 -1979 **LAW SCHOOL, UNIVERSITY OF FLORIDA, COLLEGE OF LAW**

1971 -1976 **TEACHER, PHILADELPHIA SCHOOL DISTRICT,**
PHILADELPHIA, PA. Taught English and U.S. Government, middle and
high school

RONALD DUBBELD
3167 Starway St.
Baker, Nevada , 59881
(605) 489-1264

VOLUNTEER SERVICE:

PATHFINDERS MENTORING PROGRAM - Sponsored by Kappa Alpha Psi, Omega Psi Phi and Alpha Phi Alpha fraternities, St. Petersburg, FL.

SOCIAL SERVICES - Worked with the director in subsidized housing (consultant).

CAMPAIGN MANAGER - For elected member of Atlantic City School Board. I worked the election polls/city elections, Atlantic City, NJ.

COUNSELOR - Counseled women living in a residential shelter for women with children, Atlantic City, NJ.

ATLANTIC CITY FREE (PUBLIC) LIBRARY - Historical section - Circulation spokesman on a promotional video. I received two gift awards for service.

ATLANTIC CITY FAMILY CENTER - Established and coordinated the first African-American for the Future male mentoring program.

CAMPAIGN MANAGER - For elected member of Springhill City School Board. I worked the election polls/city elections, Springhill, NJ.

COUNSELOR - Counseled women living in a residential shelter for women with children, Springhill, NJ.

BRITT HOUSE - Juvenile Detention Center, Springhill, NJ. Bible study, life skills, sponsored by St. Augustine Episcopal Church.

WEED AND SEED, CITY OF SPRINGHILL, NJ - Prevention, Intervention and Treatment subcommittee.

Susan had injured her back and needed to get into something other than direct care nursing. She stressed her education and duties related to the fields in which she was targeting.

SUSAN POWELL
8707 Wedgewood Drive
Memphis, Tennessee 75219
(489) 355-4519

OBJECTIVE: *Professional Opportunity in Nursing Quality Assurance, Utilization Review, Risk-Case Management, Legal Case Review*

PROFILE: Nursing professional with Operative, Wound Care, Medical Photography, and Medical Record management experience

EDUCATION: Nova University - Master's program - Psychology
Bachelor's of Arts in Psychology and Bachelor's of Science, University of Kentucky, Louisville, KY
Phi Beta Kappa, QPB
Alpha of Kentucky in recognition of high attainment in liberal scholarship

LICENSES: State of Florida Registered Nurse Professional

CERTIFICATIONS: Operating Room Skills for RNs - FL Dept. of Education

1999-2001 **Ambulatory Surgery Center**, Tampa, Florida
Operating Room, R.N.
- Surgical assisting
- Chart review
- Instrument sterilization
- Operative room and supply preparation
- Record management

1995-1999 **Charles McLaughlin, M.D.,** Tampa, Florida
Office R.N.
- Medical photography
- Wound care
- Patient education
- Chart review

HOBBIES: Reading, antiques, sports

James was no longer able to work as a truck driver due to a left knee injury. Even though his dispatching experience was secondary to his driving experience, he did have the skills needed to do the job.

JAMES BLACKWELL

1265 Bay St.
Detroit, Michigan 34564
Ph: (730) 344-2888

OBJECTIVE: DISPATCHING

PROFILE: Responsible and hard-working individual with extensive knowledge of Detroit and State of Michigan roads seeking a challenging job with room for advancement.

SUMMARY OF QUALIFICATIONS:

- Radio dispatching
- Computer dispatching – Qualcom
- Computer literate – Windows, Word, Excel, Internet
- General office skills – Multi-line phones, 10 key, fax, etc.
- Adept at handling emergencies and maintaining calm disposition
- Strong mechanical aptitude
- Proven customer service skills

PROFESSIONAL EXPERIENCE:

2001-2002   **Pro-One Drivers,** Detroit, MI, <u>Truck driver</u>
Haz-Mat, refrigeration, tankers, extra-wides, semi tractor-trailers
- Local and OTR deliveries

1998-2001   **Stanley Leasing**, Lansing, MI, <u>Truck Driver</u>
- Picked up and loaded trailers delivering to Scotty's stores in Michigan
- Assigned and dispatched loads to 25 drivers
- Maintained radio contact – handling questions, emergencies, and customer service

1994-1998   **Blackwell and Sons Trucking**, Detroit, MI, <u>Owner/Operator</u>
- Over the Road Driver covering 48 states

EDUCATION: Delta High School, Detroit, Michigan
Lakeland Senior High School – High School Graduate

VOLUNTEER ACTIVITIES:
1980-1990   **Tooga County Fire District #2**, Tooga, MI, <u>Volunteer Firefighter</u>,
Started as Lieutenant and promoted to Assistant Chief

Woman Returning to Workforce

Marcia had been out of the workforce for many years. She was quite active as a volunteer. Since she was looking for work in the field of social services, we stressed her education and volunteer experience.

MARCIA GOLDFARB
560 Winding Creek Drive , Pittsburgh, PA
Phone: (727) 392-5858
Email: mgold@earthlink.com

OBJECTIVE: HUMAN SERVICES - CASE MANAGER - COUNSELOR

PROFILE: Resourceful communicator with extensive experience working with youth, adults, families, terminally ill, low-income, volunteers, and fundraising

EDUCATION: **Bachelor's of Science in Human Services,** University Of Scranton, PA; Drama/Psychology, Ithaca College, Ithaca, NY

SUMMARY OF QUALIFICATIONS
- Experienced educator and mentor
- Elderly and terminally ill medical case management
- Volunteer and student coordination
- Proven leadership and communication skills
- Adept at relating with persons of all levels and diverse cultures

COMMUNITY SERVICE:
- Volunteered at Seminole Middle School placing mentors with students, 1999-2001
- Participated in senior visitation program, visiting elderly in nursing homes, hospitals
- Girl Scouts, co-scout leader: activity planning, leadership and fundraising, 1994-1999
- Student Teaching: Learning-Disabled Classes through drama activities

PROFESSIONAL EXPERIENCE:

AMERICAN SECURITY SERVICES, Pittsburgh, PA, 12 years
Part-time Office Manager
- Managed elderly customers inquiries, complaints and confusion
- Referred families and individuals to community resources

MEDLINE SERVICES, Philadelphia, PA, 12 years
Supervisor/Centralized Underwriting Medical History Department
- Managed staff of 15 doctors and nurses to obtain medical histories for the purpose of underwriting insurance policies
- Responsible for medical reviews and clarifying physician recommendations
- Hiring, training, and motivating personnel
- Obtained, reviewed, and clarified medical histories for underwriting

BUREAU OF EMPLOYMENT SECURITY, Scranton, PA, 3 years
Unemployment Compensation Claims Taker
- Interviewed the unemployed and determined eligibility for state unemployment

In this resume, we stressed Marcia's work experience, which directly related to the position that she was seeking in the medical insurance field.

MARCIA GOLDFARB
560 Winding Creek Drive, Pittsburg, PA
Phone: (727) 392-5858
Email: mgold@@earthlink.com

OBJECTIVE: **Position in Medical Office using my ability to relate to people, medical and insurance background, and willingness to learn.**

PROFILE: Resourceful communicator with extensive experience working with youth, adults, families, terminally ill, low income, volunteers, and fundraising

EDUCATION: **Bachelor's of Science in Human Services,** University Of Scranton, PA; Drama/Psychology, Ithaca College, Ithaca, NY

SUMMARY OF QUALIFICATIONS
- Knowledge of medical terminology and medical procedures
- Claims processing and medical record-keeping
- Tenacious and thorough
- Adept at communicating with persons of all levels and diverse cultures

PROFESSIONAL EXPERIENCE:
AMERICAN SECURITY SERVICES, Pittsburgh, PA, 12 years
Part-time Office Manager
- Managed elderly customers inquiries, complaints and confusion
- Referred families and individuals to community resources

MEDLINE SERVICES, Philadelphia, PA, 12 years
Supervisor, Centralized Underwriting Medical History Department
- Managed staff of 15 doctors and nurses to obtain medical histories for the purpose of underwriting insurance policies
- Responsible for medical review and clarifying physician recommendations
- Hiring, training, and motivating personnel
- Obtained, reviewed, and clarified medical histories for underwriting

BUREAU OF EMPLOYMENT SECURITY, Scranton, PA, 3 years
Unemployment Compensation Claims Taker
- Interviewed the unemployed and determined eligibility for state unemployment benefits.
- Made referrals to community resources for assistance

COMMUNITY SERVICE:
- Volunteered at Seminole Middle School placing mentors with students, 1999-2001
- Girl Scouts, co-scout leader: Activity planning, leadership and fundraising, 1994-1999

Clyde could no longer perform the physical duties of an electrician. Building on his electrician's skills, he returned to school to learn drafting. With this resume, he was hired at an engineering firm. They were thrilled that he had practical experience in both industrial maintenance and construction.

CLYDE WOODS
45 Hollow Road
Paloma, CA 52019
(410) 481-1114

OBJECTIVE: AUTOCAD or ATD Drafting/Architectural or Mechanical

QUALIFICATIONS:
- Auto/CAD 2002
- Architectural Desktop 3.3
- Strong Mechanical and Electronic Background
- Familiar with government specs and processes
- 2002 Principal's Honor Roll - 4.0 GPA - National Vocational Technical Honor Society
- 1998 Principal's Honor Roll - 4.0 GPA - National Vocational Technical Honor Society

CERTIFICATIONS:
Drafting/AutoCAD - 08/2001 - 03/2003, Paloma Technical Center, Paloma, CA
Industrial Electricity - 01/1997 - 01/1998, Lansing Technical Institute, Lansing, MI

PROFESSIONAL EXPERIENCE:
8/2003 - current   **DAPPER DESIGN**
                Auto/CAD Tech (Temporary Independent Contractor)
- Architectural drafting

4/1998-4/2000   **PRO-ELECTRIC**
                Apprentice Electrician
- Residential, commercial, and industrial Wiring

1/1982-6/1996   **RAYTHEON CO.**
                QA Refrigeration and Hydraulic Repair Technician
- Maintained and repaired test equipment involving water chillers, pumping stations, and environmental chambers

                QA Mechanical Calibrator
- Periodic calibration of pressure gauges, measuring devices, environmental chambers, and torque devices

                Hydraulic Tester
- Tested hydraulic hoses, fittings, and pressure connectors

                Printed Wiring Fabrication Inspector
- Visual and mechanical inspection of printed wiring boards

Immigrant   Although Ivan was licensed as an architect in the Ukraine, he did not have any relevant work experience in the United States. His skills were also outdated, prompting him to return to school to learn AutoCad. While attending school, he did some freelance work, which gave him credibility and local experience.

IVAN DASTEK
2020 Target Avenue, Flint, MA
Phone (898) 218-4456

SUMMARY: **Sixteen years as a practicing architect**
Project management experience
Design and supervision experience on large projects
Working knowledge of standard building codes in United States
Certification in Auto CAD 2002, Architectural Desktop 3.3,
3D Studio VIZ 3, 3DSMAX 4

EXPERIENCE   **Dortan Concepts,** Flint, MA: **PRESIDENT & OWNER**
1995-Currently

Design residential modifications and updates. Develop, design and monitor a project for an Assisted Living Facility in St. Petersburg, FL. Inventory and redesign commercial properties to accommodate changes in use for a major commercial developer. Generate reports on utilization of properties including drafting of all floor plans and elevations.

1990-1994   **Matori,** Intivka, Ukraine: **DIRECTOR**

Founded a company under the new economic system after the breakup of the Soviet Union. Managed all contracts for services by the company. Supervised a staff of ten architects and monitored all of the projects undertaken. Developed business contacts with Poland, Germany, and other non-bloc countries. Expanded business to included educational facilities, resorts, multi-family dwellings, student unions, and other large projects.

1986-1990   **Student Project Construction Bureau,** Intirka, Ukraine:
                      CHIEF ARCHITECT

Designed and developed a 78-unit apartment complex, including landscape design. Supervised teams of architects the development of projects for public and private sectors to include public and residential use.

EDUCATION: 2003 Certification in AutoCAD, Flint Community College, Flint, MA
Five-year degree in Architecture, L'viv Polytechnic Institute, L'viv, Ukraine, 1981

PROFESSIONAL   Ukrainian Association of Architects

Ethnic Discrimination

Balia's qualifications were strong, so we highlighted specific action verbs to provide visual interest and to emphasize her strengths. Unfortunately, she was looking for work after 9/11, and in light of her heritage, employers were hesitant to consider her. Although Arabic was her first language, to minimize discrimination we did not include that on her resume.

Balia Abdour _____ **(409) 352-3399**

OBJECTIVE: Seeking a challenging position incorporating my experience in **coding, testing,** and **debugging** in UNIX, C and C++ in 5ESS systems

EDUCATION: Post-graduate Technical Courses, AT&T/Lucent, Naperville, IL

Advanced System Overview	UNIX Shell
Software Architecture, Data Base C, C++	
Call Processing, BRCS	Fortran IV
Translations & Element	Object/time
Collection Techniques	HTML
Work Effectiveness	Perl
International Marketing	COBOL
SDE - ECMS	JAVA

Computer Science Degree: 96 credit hours, Union County College, Scotch Plains, NJ
Computers & Operators Degree: School of Data Programming, Union, NJ
Accounting Degree, B.S.: Alexandria Faculty of Commerce, Alexandria, Egypt

EXPERIENCE:
1998 - 2000   **Shop at Home,** Testing and Debugging
Planned, executed and tracked regression and system tests for phone ordering system.

1995 - 1998   **Lucent Technologies,** Naperville, IL. - Testing and Debugging (Consultant)

5ESS EXPERIENCE: Planned, executed, and tracked regression and feature tests including C based program for OSPS including TCS, VMS, LNP and SS7. Created a manual, using HTML, which documents procedures for lab bring-up and testing operations

Advanced Services Operations System Experience: Created, coordinated, and executed automated and non-automated pairwise tests, including C & C++ based programs using the CMIP for the following features: Dispatch Management, Field Access, MPM, PPM, Physical Net Working, Data Management and Host Digital Terminal Element Manager, and Loop Surveillance.

LANGUAGES: English and French.

Notice how Mr. Williams' accomplishments emphasize his ability to generate and close sales.

JOE WILLIAMS
P.O. Box 3511
Raleigh, NC 22337
Ph: (360) 398- 9638

SEEKING: SALES MANAGEMENT or **ACCOUNT REPRESENTATIVE** where my relationship building and analytical skills can make a significant difference

EXPERIENCE:

GOURMET COFFEES OF FLORIDA, St. Petersburg, Florida, 1985 - 1999
<u>Sales Manager</u>
¢Responsible for establishing retail locations and wholesale coffee sales for company that purchased, packaged, and distributed gourmet coffee
¢Trained and managed outside and retail sales teams
¢Negotiated profitable state and municipal contracts for coffee distribution

*Accomplishments: Increased sales from **$150m to 2.8mm** in three years; expanded company from one storefront into franchised operation; established cooperative relationship with competitors to package their coffee products in private label program.*

INTERNATIONAL PAPER CO., Bagpack Division, New York, 1980-1985
<u>International Sales Representative</u>, Fortune 100 Company
¢Responsible for corporate sales of multi-wall packaging to chemical, agricultural, and building industries
¢Serviced Georgia and Florida territories and managed expansion of sales into Caribbean and South American markets
¢Interviewed and trained sales force

Accomplishments: Developed network of brokers and dealers leading to substantial increase of sales volume.

CALITRON ULTRASONICS, Jacksonville, Florida, 1979-1980
<u>Sales and Marketing</u> of customized capital equipment utilized in bonding and welding thermoplastics to manufacturing, electronic, and medical industries
¢Utilizing sales forecasting, market analysis and research
¢Developed Caribbean and Puerto Rico Territories
¢Formulated and implemented direct mail and marketing programs

EDUCATION: UNIVERSITY OF TAMPA, Tampa, Florida
Masters of Business Administration

Mailroom—Temp to Perm

William had moved from New York to Miami when I met him. His specialty was processing and preparing large mailings. He had been out of work over a year, but he was able to cover the gap by focusing on his skills. As he had previously been successful in getting hired at large corporations through staffing services, he signed with several agencies in the Miami area and soon was working "temp to perm" for a large retail chain's mail department. He is not earning quite as much as he did in New York City, but he does love the good weather.

William Dartmouth
626 42nd St. North
Miami, Fl 33760
(727) 532-3077

Objective: Seeking a Mailroom / Clerical position.

Skills: Paragon 2500; Fedex PowerShip II/III; UPS; Xerox Docutect 2500, 5200, and 5280 equipment; PowerPoint; Windows 9x; MS Word; Excel; Internet and E-mail Applications; customer service.

Experience: **Fairway Holdings, Inc.**, New York, 4/00 - 4/02
Fulfillment Clerk (7/00 to 4/02)

Entered information into computer to prepare marketing materials for conferences; managed inventory of all marketing supplies, promotions, and giveaways and ordered from printer/manufacturer; shipped out diverse marketing materials to clients on a daily basis; input data into PowerPoint presentations; sorted and filed records; maintained and operated Xerox Docutect 2500, 5200, 5280 equipment; addressed envelopes and packages by hand and typewriter; bound presentation books and photocopied documents; answered telephones, conveyed messages and ran errands; expedited communication between upper level management and general personnel; stamped, sorted, and distributed mail.

Mailroom Clerk (4/00 to 7/00)
Temporary position through Kelly Staffing Services, New York

Sorted incoming mail for distribution and dispatched outgoing mail; applied knowledge of postal rates, UPS, FedEx; opened envelopes by hand and machine; stamped date and time of receipt on incoming mail; executed daily operations of stamping mail, sorting mail, delivering UPS and FedEx packages and messenger packages; responsible for late afternoon pickup of mail, closing out UPS and FedEx machines; maintained supplies; weighed mail to determine correct postage; kept record of registered mail.

A-I International Services, Union, New Jersey
Mailroom Clerk, 9/98 to 2/00

Sorted incoming mail for distribution and dispatched outgoing mail; examined outgoing mail for appearance and sealed envelopes by machine; stamped date and time of receipt on incoming mail; stamped mail using addressing machine; operated the folding machine that processed advertising literature, forms, letters, and other paper sheets; distributed and collected mail; weighed mail to determine correct postage; kept record of registered mail.

Education: James High School, Bronx, New York, HS Diploma, 1985

Getting Started On Your Resume

Now that you've studied some samples, let's begin building your own sample resume here. Complete the blanks. Remember to stress your strengths. The next few pages will go into detail on how best to fill in each section.

NAME
Address
City, State, Zip
Telephone   E-mail:

OBJECTIVE:

PROFILE:

SUMMARY OF QUALIFICATIONS:
-
-
-
-

WORK HISTORY:

19__ - 20__

_____

-
-

Accomplishments:

19__ - 19__

_____

-
-

19__ - 19__

_____

-
-

EDUCATION:

MILITARY:

PROFESSIONAL LICENSES:

COMMUNITY INVOLVEMENT:

HOBBIES:

(References available upon request)

OBJECTIVE: *Your objective is your targeted job goal.*

Example:

OBJECTIVE: Construction Supervisor

If you are unsure as to exactly what type of job you are looking for, use a more general objective. To create a more general objective, use words from the section *What do I need from my job*?

What is your ideal work environment?
☑ Challenging work
☑ Room for growth
☑Large company

Example:

OBJECTIVE: A challenging position in large company with potential for growth.

PROFILE: Use your answers from the section *Getting to Know You:*

☑ Competent   ☑ Energetic
☑ Dependable   ☑ Diplomatic
☑ Persistent

Or use your answers from the section *What Interests You?*

☑ Mathematics
☑ Helping people
☑ Managing people

Example:

PROFILE: A competent and dependable worker who is good with numbers and enjoys working with people.

Or:

PROFILE: An energetic, diplomatic and persistent professional with fifteen years of experience in the construction industry.

A profile creates an image so that the prospective employer begins to know you.

SUMMARY OF QUALIFICATIONS: Use your transferable skills and any other skills that you may have acquired through hobbies, taking care of your family or in a class.

Example:

In your previous job as a carpenter you measured and cut wood and metal products, used tools including hammers, saws, nails, and screws.

Skills:

Read blueprints
Lay out a floor plan
Supervise workers
Purchase materials
Estimate costs
Knowledge of building codes and inspection procedures.
Use hand tools
Measure accurately.
Closing sales
Customer Service

Quantify your skills. Include the following details about your skills:

How much?

How many?

What kind?

Where?

Example:

OBJECTIVE: Construction Sales and Estimating

PROFILE: An energetic, diplomatic and persistent professional with fifteen years experience in the construction industry.

SUMMARY OF QUALIFICATIONS:

- Knowledge of materials and labor costs for framing, trim, and flooring
- Estimating experience in new and remodels up to $250,000
- Able to read blueprints and lay out floor plans
- Knowledge of building codes and inspection procedures
- Ability to measure accurately
- Excellent at closing sales and customer service

Or:

OBJECTIVE: Construction Supervisor

PROFILE: A competent and dependable worker who is good with numbers and enjoys working with people.

SUMMARY OF QUALIFICATIONS:

- Supervised crews of up to ten workers
- Purchased materials for job sites
- Able to manage multiple job sites simultaneously
- Estimate labor costs for projects up to $250,000
- Knowledge of building codes and inspection procedures
- Familiar with local vendors, distributors, carpenters, and laborers
- Customer-friendly

Use information from your application.

Example:

WORK HISTORY:

19__ - 20__

_____

- •
- •
- •

Accomplishments:

19__ - 19__

_____

- •
- •
- •

19__ - 19__

_____

- •
- •

Or:

If you have a long work history or have a lot of gaps in your work history, simply list the related work history *without* the dates.

Example:

RELATED WORK HISTORY:

- • Ten years experience working with ABC Tools in purchasing
- • Five years experience as a sales clerk at Buy Rite Furniture

NAME
Address
City, State, Zip
Telephone   E-mail:

OBJECTIVE:

PROFILE:

SUMMARY OF QUALIFICATIONS:
-
-
-
-

WORK HISTORY:

19__ - 20__

_____
-
-

Accomplishments:

19__ - 19__

_____
-
-

19__ - 19__

_____
-
-

EDUCATION:

MILITARY:

PROFESSIONAL LICENSES:

COMMUNITY INVOLVEMENT:

HOBBIES:

(References available upon request)

Do I need a cover letter?

No, not if it keeps you from sending out your resume.

A cover letter can take different forms:

→ A fax sheet

→ A standard cover letter

→ An e-mail

→ A personal cover letter that addresses a specific person and identifies the job for which you are applying

→ A detailed cover letter that describes your particular circumstances and explains why you would like to work for this company

A note regarding cover letters:

While most career books stress the importance of a cover letter, I have been quite successful in faxing my clients' resumes with just a fax sheet that includes a written note. In light of my high placement rate, I can honestly say that this technique has been quite effective.

Unless a cover letter includes information vital to the job duties or information that cannot easily be conveyed on a resume, a cover letter serves little purpose, except to address and direct the attached resume to a specific person.

Nonetheless, for high-end positions that may include several interviews and many different persons reviewing the resume, cover letters *can* help the interviewers get to know you and give them an indication of how you present yourself to others.

→ TIP: If you are faxing to multiple companies on the same day, *write the contact information in pencil.* You can erase the names and numbers and keep the rest of the information. This goes quite quickly and *gets your resume in front of more people.*

The next few pages present examples of different types of cover letters that may be attached *with your resume*. You may decide to use one of these examples as a model for your own cover letter.

Fax Cover Letter:

Bill Thompson
9100 Main Street.
St. Petersburg, Florida 33712
(727) 956-0199

Fax

To:	Brad Leffers c/o Inway Industries	**From:** Paula Vieillet
Fax:	(813) 931 - 1212	**Date:**
Phone:	(813) 931 - 1265	**Pages:** 2
Re:	Customer service	**cc:**

☐ **Urgent**   ☐ **For Review**   ☐ **Please Comment**   ☐ **Please Reply**

Comments:

Dear Mr. Leffers,

Thanks for taking a look. Feel free to call me with any questions.

Sincerely,

Bill Thompson

Beverly Hanes
8901 Floral Dr.
Springfield, MO
Tel/Fax: (405) 822-3211   Cell: (405) 320-6053

September 10, 2008

_____(Insert Name Here)_____, Department of Human Resources
(Insert Street Address and Inside Address)
(Insert City, State, and Zip Code)

Dear (Insert Name Here):

Thank you much for considering me for your auditor position. I have been working for Clayton County as a (insert current job title here). However, since this position was not a permanent position, I would be interested in finding out more about your position at (insert prospective employer name here).

I would love the opportunity to use my education in a government position where I can be of service to our country.

Sincerely,

Beverly Hanes

WALTER SIMMONS
10692 Turkey Creek Drive
Arlington, VA
(680) 725-9932

February 10, 2009

_____(Insert Name Here)_____, Department of Human Resources
(Insert Street Address and Inside Address)
(Insert City, State, and Zip Code)

Dear (Insert Name Here):

Thank you very much for considering me for your accounting position. As you can see from my resume, I have over 10 years of experience in a human resource environment. My resume is attached for your convenience.

Sincerely,

Walter Simmons

JANE BASSET
7490 Southside Blvd.
Jacksonville, Florida 32256
(850) 983-9855

March 19, 2009

_____(Insert Name Here)_____, Department of Human Resources
(Insert Street Address and Inside Address)
(Insert City, State, and Zip Code)

To Whom It May Concern:

Thank you for considering my candidature for the position of program assistant.

Having just graduated in International Relations, I feel that my education, as well as my personal experience, would lend itself to the duties specified in this position.

Sincerely,

Jane Basset

Notice that Nicole addressed this letter to a particular person instead of "To Whom It May Concern."

NICOLE BRENTFIELD
7125 Nickelback Rd.
Anycity, FL 34409
Ph: (727) 743-4413
e-mail: Nb4114@hotmail.com

Brenda Watkins
c/o Sea Port Aquarium
8888 Sea Port Lane
Sea Port, Florida 99999

Dear Ms. Watkins:

I am applying for the position of aquarist. With my marine background, I feel that I would be well suited to this position. Attached is my resume for your review.

I would appreciate the opportunity to speak with you further regarding this opportunity. Thank you for your consideration.

Sincerely,

Nicole Brentfield

John Tanner
8119 W. Willow Ave.
Chicago, Ill. 98894
E-mail: jtann@aol.com

Jane Willow
c/o Mane Corporation
2222 Main Street
Chicago, Ill. 98339

Date

Dear Ms. Willow,

I am interested in exploring management positions with your construction company. In my last position I managed a crew of ten and was responsible for managing labor costs, ordering materials, and budgeting.

As I am finding that carpentry only uses some of my abilities, I am looking for a management opportunity that will challenge me.

Thank you so much for your consideration. I would love the opportunity to help your company increase productivity and profits.

Sincerely,

John Tanner

TOM DUNCAN
1311 Bohemia Way
St. Petersburg, FL 31227
(813) 863-3809

March 19, 2009

Department of Human Resources

To Whom It May Concern:

I am interested in exploring management positions in your calling center operations. Due to a recent reorganization at Priment, I have recently been laid-off from a management position.

My preference is to remain working in the Tampa Bay Region, where my extensive experience in high-volume calling can be utilized.

Sincerely,

Tom Duncan

RANDOLPH LOIRET
8945 Prithham Road
Boston, MA 35903
(918) 360-5828   e-mail: loiret@mindspring.com

Larry Koffman
Macy's Department Store
Perimeter Plaza
Boston, MA

August 15, 2008

Dear Mr. Koffman,

Please take into account my nine years of supervisory experience, as well as extensive hands-on knowledge of investigating Workers' Compensation claims, when considering my candidacy for the position of supervisor of security.

As the manager at Brighten Insurance, I have had the pleasure of supervising professionals working in the field as well as strategically collaborating with attorneys regarding Workers' Compensation claims liability.

My military background, combined with my business experience, will ensure a security force that protects and respects. I'm looking forward to the opportunity to be of service to you.

Sincerely,

Randolph Loiret

Did They Receive Your Resume?

Follow-up is essential!

When you follow-up with a prospective
employer, your resume is
automatically placed
on the top of their stack.

Sample follow-up call:

"*Hi, could I speak to* (insert name of contact person)."
(If your contact person is unavailable, ask the person answering the phone
if they know if your resume was received.)

"*I am just checking to make sure that you received my resume.*"
(The primary purpose of this call is primarily to see if they did receive
the resume, and to get it on the top of the stack.)

"*Did you have any questions?*"
(Answer any questions.)

If they are not too busy, ask, "*When do you expect to be interviewing?*"

If they are busy, just thank them, and be glad that your resume is on the top.

Luck is what happens when preparation meets opportunity.

—Seneca

Interviews

The interview is where both you and the employer learn about each other. The most successful interviews happen when you go prepared.

Being prepared means knowing a little about the company, the particular job and how your backgrounds fits into the picture.

This chapter will help you prepare for all types of interviews and negotiations. You will learn how to ask the employer questions that will show your knowledge of the industry as well as answer those questions that will help you decide if this is the right type of job for you.

Preparing For the Interview

Are your ready? *(Check off each item as you go.)*

☐ Special grooming: polished shoes, hair styled, nails appropriate length

☐ Clean clothing, work/interview appropriate; no open-toe shoes

☐ Completed practice application with names and dates for previous employers, references, and schools

☐ Two forms of identification

☐ Supplemental information, like Letters of Recommendation

☐ Information about company or job description

☐ Name of the person who will be interviewing you

☐ Date and time of interview

☐ Knowledge of possible reasonable accommodations

First Impressions

How you walk in, sit, and position yourself during an interview speaks as loudly as your words. In fact, it is usually the first impression that counts the most. Your "body language" subconsciously expresses our attitudes.

*By **consciously** adjusting you body posture, a change in how others perceive you is inevitable. Subconsciously, your own attitudes will change as you work to express a more positive body posture. Below is a list of basic body postures and the attitudes they convey:*

Cooperative: Relaxed body, no furrows on forehead, friendly greeting, open stance

Lack of Confidence: Head down, slumped posture, slow pace, difficulty sustaining eye contact*

Enthusiastic/Confident: Puts weight on balls of feet, sits toward the end of the chair, posture erect, chin up, tilted head, relaxed forehead

Hostile/Defensive: Arms crossed, intense and glaring eyes, hands clenched, tight facial features

Impatient: Taps foot, shifts positions frequently, looks away*, fidgets with hands

Lying: Does not make good eye contact*, looks away when speaking, puts hands in front of mouth

Control: Tight lips, leans forward, closer than normal "comfort zone," hands on thighs

Frustration: Short breathing, restless hands, pushes air through nose, tense body posture, eyes squinting*

Accepting: Head slightly nodding up and down, arms at sides and body leaning a little backward in chair, mouth smiling

In some cultures, **not making eye contact is the norm in an interview situation. In the United States (unless your job will be **located** in another culture), making eye contact is **essential** to a good interview.*

Typical Interview Questions

Writing will help you think through your answers to these questions before you go to a job interview. If possible, have someone practice with you or practice out loud. *Write down your responses to the following questions.*

▶ **Tell me about the work that you performed with your previous company.**

Try to match your previous skills with skills needed in this position.

▶ **What did you like about working there?**

Once again try to make the connection, if possible, from your old job to the new job.

For example: A route sales driver applying for a customer service position might say, *I liked serving the customers.*

▶ **Why did you leave your last job?**

For example: *I wanted more opportunity for advancement.*

Or: *The job was no longer appropriate, as it involved too much lifting/typing/ standing.*

▶ **Tell me about your other jobs.**

Talk about related skills.

▶ **Why is there a gap in your employment?**

I took some time off, but I am ready to go back to work.

► What was your most challenging task at your previous employment?

Pick something related to the new job, and talk about how you overcame this obstacle.

► What are your major strengths?

Use those strength words!

► What are your major weaknesses?

You can also use your strength words here. Try to match your weaknesses with the job.

For example: *I tend to be too meticulous;* Or, *Sometimes I'm too independent.*

► What hours can you work?

Be honest but flexible!

► What do you like to do in your spare time?

Mention your hobbies.

► Are you able to perform the essential functions of the position with or without reasonable accommodations?

*If you can do the job – even if you need accommodations – say **YES**.*

► How do you think you would like working here?

Show you are motivated. Be enthusiastic!

► **What was your biggest accomplishment in your last job?**

Pick something related to the prospective job. You may have saved the company money, or perhaps you used your supervisory and organizational skills to get a project finished ahead of schedule.

► **What would your ideal job be?**

Try to show them how the job they are hiring for is related to your ideal job. Maybe you love to work with people, and the job involves customer service.

► **How would your friends and family describe you?**

Usually their descriptions of you will be somewhat comparable to your own list. You can prepare for this question by asking a few people to describe you.

► **Why should I hire you?**

Be able to answer this question confidently! You should know how your skills and abilities will benefit the company.

► **How do you think you can make a contribution to our business?**

Explain how you saved or made money for your last employer. For example, if you are applying for an attorney position, you could talk about a case that you successfully negotiated.

► **What are your long-term and short-term goals?**

Match your goals with company goals. Many companies describe their goals on their web site. Look for their mission statement.

Answering Difficult Interview Questions

You can expect to be asked some tough questions in any job interview. Below are examples of some of the tough questions you may face and some possible responses to those questions.

Why have you been off work for so long?

▶ I had some personal challenges, but now I am ready and able to get the job done.

▶ We had a family member who needed extra care, so I took some time off to do that. *(The family member can be you!)*

▶ Although I was not working in paid employment, I did a lot of volunteering. I learned a lot about _____, which should be very helpful in this job.

▶ I had an opportunity to take time off, but now I am ready and motivated to return to work.

When answering a tough question, address the concern, and steer the interviewer back to your interest in the job.

This job pays a lot less than your previous job.

▶ I loved making a lot of money, but my priorities have changed. I would prefer to work in a field that I love rather than stay in something that I do not like just for money.

▶ Unfortunately, most of the jobs I had in the past are no longer available or in demand in our job market, and I would prefer not to move.

▶ I am aware of that, but I have to start somewhere. I have adjusted my spending to accommodate a lower salary.

▶ It is more than I am making now, and I look forward to learning more about what you do here.

▶ Coming from a different career field, I did not think I would start at the top, but as long as there is room for advancement, I am a fast learner, and I would be willing to show you what I can do.

▶ I am flexible with wages. Learning something new is more important to me than salary.

After the Interview

How did you do? *Check all that apply.*

- ☐ Arrived on time for the interview
- ☐ Brought a pen, examples of your work, and an extra copy of your resume
- ☐ Presented skills and abilities in a positive fashion
- ☐ Smiled
- ☐ Refrained from "bad-mouthing" previous employers
- ☐ Shared relevant information with prospective employer
- ☐ Answered interview questions appropriately, sticking to the question and not giving out too much unrelated information
- ☐ Asked appropriate questions about job duties and employer's expectations
- ☐ Showed enthusiasm
- ☐ Used appropriate body language: shaking hands, making good eye contact
- ☐ Did not try to extend the interview when the interviewer indicated that it was over
- ☐ Thanked the employer for the interview
- ☐ Set a timeframe to find out if you have been hired for the job
- ☐ Got the name of the interviewer
- ☐ Increased your knowledge of the company, its philosophies, work hours, benefits, and job responsibilities
- ☐ Sent a personal note to thank the employer for the interview

Follow-up also lets employers know that you are interested in the job and that you want the opportunity to work for them.

An average of six contacts with an employer is necessary to be hired for the job. Any initial contact, interview, or follow-up counts.

Don't give up until you have a definite six.

	1st contact	2nd contact
Employer or contact person		
Date		
Type of follow-up		
Results		

	3rd contact	4th contact
Employer or contact person		
Date		
Type of follow-up		
Results		

	5th contact	6th contact
Employer or contact person		
Date		
Type of follow-up		
Results		

Referrals

1.

2.

3.

Comments

1.

2.

3.

Different Types Of Follow-up

> There are various methods for following up after your interview, but the basic principle is this: keep it brief and simple. Use the examples below as possible models for your own follow-up.

Thank-You Note or Card

Example:
Dear _____,
Thank you for taking the time to interview me last (<u>day of week</u>) for the position of _____.
I enjoyed meeting you and learning about your company. I look forward to talking with you again soon regarding the opportunity to work for your company.
Sincerely,

Telephone Call

Example:
Hello, is (<u>name of the person you had the interview with</u>) there? This is (<u>your name</u>). I interviewed with you last (<u>day of week</u>) and I am calling to follow-up, to determine if you had a chance to make a decision regarding the position of _____?
Am I catching you at a bad time?

In Person

Example:
In-person follow-up is not necessarily the best type. It is mostly appropriate if you have some additional information, such as a letter of reference or a work sample to drop off, which might have an impact on being hired. Go at a time when the employer would generally not be busy. It is **not** appropriate to drop in during their rush hour. Do not stay too long.

How many times do I have to interview?

How many times you interview depends on the employer's policies. Some employers always have two interviews; other employers may only interview you once. Depending on the company, some job seekers may have three or four interviews.

They want to schedule me for a telephone interview.

Telephone interviews are becoming more common. Be sure to schedule it at a time when you can give the interviewer your full attention. Make arrangements for your children to be occupied at that time. Have your resume with you by the phone. Although they cannot see you, they can hear your voice. Speak enthusiastically. Use your best telephone manners.

I am going to a group interview.

Group interviews, where the employer interviews more than one applicant at a time, may be a bit intimidating and impersonal, but for employers, it gives them a chance to meet a lot of people in a short amount of time. Group interviews are most common when an employer will be hiring a number of people. Stay calm. Do your best.

I am going to be interviewed by a panel.

Employers use panel interviews for positions that may interact with various departments or for professional-level jobs. Try to find out who will be on the panel and what their roles are in the company.

They offered me a job, but I am not sure if I want to take it.

It is perfectly fine to ask for a little time to make a decision. You may want to talk to your spouse or to a friend before you accept the job. You may want to take a look at the job description before you accept. You may want a higher starting salary. Set a time when you will get back with the employer. At that point, you should be ready to either turn down the offer or negotiate it.

You Have Been Offered a Job!

> **NOW is the time to discuss terms and details of the job offer.**

Common areas of negotiation are:

1. **Salary**

2. **Benefits**

   - **Health Insurance:** You may have a choice of health plans

   - **Vacation:** Depending on your expertise, you may be able to negotiate days

   - **Sick time:** This is usually standard for all employees

   - **Holidays**: Companies usually offer some paid holidays

   - **Flex-time:** Some companies offer flex-time instead of vacation and sick time

   - **Short-term disability**: Some employers offer it as a paid benefit; others may offer it but not contribute to the costs

   - **Long-term disability**: Usually offered at the employee cost

   - **Profit-sharing:** Not all companies offer

   - **Parking:** If you work downtown, this may be an important item to discuss

3. **Hours**

   - What shift will you be working?

   - Will you punch a clock?

   - Is there much overtime?

   - What will you be paid for overtime?

   - Can you vary your hours to better fit your needs?

4. Job duties

It is not a bad idea to ask for a job description, if they have one, so that you have a better idea of what will be expected of you.

5. Dress

- Will you be wearing a uniform?
- Do they supply the uniforms?
- What about laundering uniforms?
- Are there any policies regarding jewelry, hair, jeans, facial hair, or clothing?

6. Accommodations

- Hours
- Job Duties
- Equipment

NOTE: If there is something that you absolutely need before your first day on the job, then it is a good idea to negotiate for it when you accept the job offer.

However, if you need something like a special chair or keyboard, I would wait until you use their actual set-up. Many times, employers already use some ergonomic equipment. You can negotiate accommodations at anytime.

The Job Is Yours. Congratulations!

How are you feeling?

☐ Happy

☐ Scared

☐ Excited

☐ Anxious

☐ Fearful

☐ Relieved

All of these feelings are normal after being offered a job. People are generally happy to find a job, yet scared they might not know how to do the job, or worried that they might not fit in.

Training is a normal part of any new job. It is expected that you will need to learn the procedures at your new place of work.

It is possible that you will not fit in at first. It takes a little time to build workplace relationships, but the employer thinks you will fit in just fine. That's why the company hired YOU !

Regarding Salary Negotiations

How much are you worth?

The Internet is a great place to compare your earnings to others working in your field. We all want higher pay, but most jobs do have an earning cap.

Find out what the going rate is in your industry and region.

All state, city and federal government agencies are required to list the salary ranges of their advertised positions. Compare that figure to your current or expected salary.

> ### Other sources of wage information include:
> **www.bls.gov**
> National Labor Market Statistics, Department of Labor, Wage and Salary Information
> **www.acinet.org**
> A national job bank from the One-Stop Career Centers

The want ads specifically asked for my salary history. How do I handle this?

When a prospective employer asks for a salary history before the interview, it is usually because they are looking for the best deal for their money.

Answer with a salary range, and let the prospective employer know that you are open to negotiation based on the specific job duties of the position.

If you respond with the lowest salary that you would possibly consider and the duties of the job are not being compensated according to the demands of the job, even though the employer thinks they are getting a deal, they will either attract an under-qualified person or be hiring a qualified person that feels underpaid. It is not always in an employers best interest to under pay employees if they want happy and satisfied employees.

When is the best time to discuss salary?

The best time to bring up salary is when you have been offered the job.

I was offered a job but the starting salary is too low. How should I handle this?

It is perfectly okay to tell the prospective employer that the salary is lower than what you expected. You can counter with the salary that is comfortable for you or ask if there are salary reviews.

If the starting wages are non-negotiable, perhaps you can ask for a few extra vacation days, a bonus, a company car, a laptop computer or flexible work hours to help compensate you for your lower salary.

Coping With Rejection

There are *many reasons* why you may *not* have been hired for the position:

▶ The boss may have a niece who needs a job.

▶ Your qualifications are not a good fit for this position.

▶ The company is promoting from within.

▶ The company may have decided to put a hold on filling the position.

▶ The interview may not have been reflective of your true abilities.

▶ Salary expectations may have differed considerably.

▶ The corporate culture of the business may be quite different from your own philosophies.

▶ Other candidates may be better qualified.

The background check may have revealed prohibitive conditions:

  ▶ Poor credit

  ▶ Criminal background

  ▶ Too many points on your driver's license

  ▶ Bad references

Coping With Job-search Stress

Rejection is common during a job search and can affect your self-esteem.
Taking extra care of yourself will help you to cope with this additional stress.

Include a least one positive activity per day.

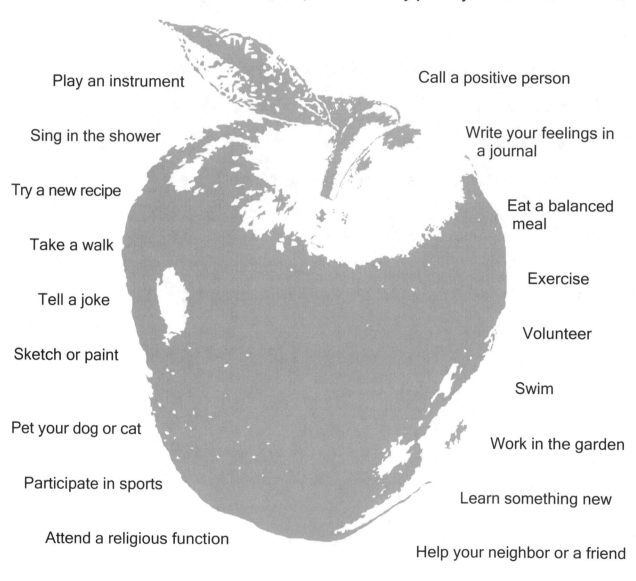

Play an instrument

Sing in the shower

Try a new recipe

Take a walk

Tell a joke

Sketch or paint

Pet your dog or cat

Participate in sports

Attend a religious function

Call a positive person

Write your feelings in
a journal

Eat a balanced
meal

Exercise

Volunteer

Swim

Work in the garden

Learn something new

Help your neighbor or a friend

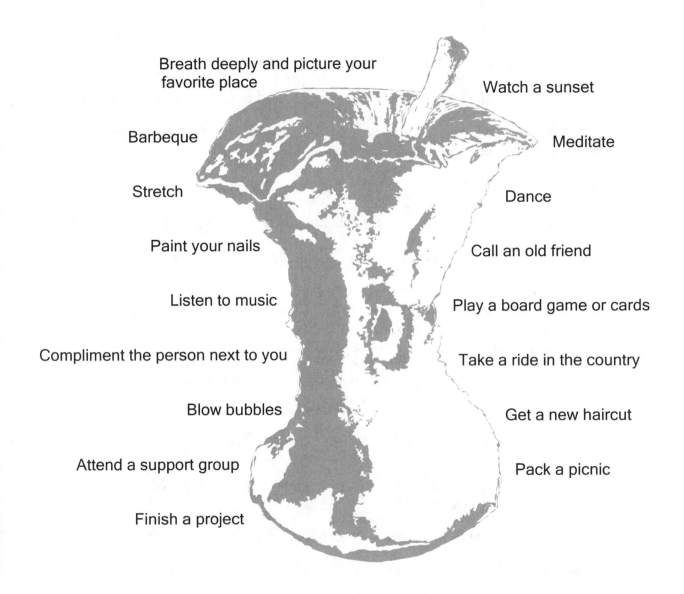

Breath deeply and picture your favorite place

Watch a sunset

Barbeque

Meditate

Stretch

Dance

Paint your nails

Call an old friend

Listen to music

Play a board game or cards

Compliment the person next to you

Take a ride in the country

Blow bubbles

Get a new haircut

Attend a support group

Pack a picnic

Finish a project

Pre-employment Testing

Psychological testing is becoming more popular as part of a job interview. These questions are among the questions that you may be asked in a job interview. These are usually multiple choice questions, and you will be asked to choose the best answer:

▶ What would you do if you saw a co-worker stealing?

▶ What would you do if you saw a customer stealing?

▶ How would you handle a situation where a co-worker was threatening you?

▶ What would you do if a customer/employee/supervisor asked you to do something against company policy/protocol?

▶ How would you handle thefts or threats by/from a supervisor?

▶ How would you handle a screaming, insistent customer/employee/supervisor?

▶ How would you handle/react to sexual advances from customer/employee/supervisor?

▶ What would you do as an employee when all assigned work has been completed? Go home? Sweep the floor? Clean up? Put your feet up and wait? Ask for more work? Get on the phone?

▶ How would you respond to a supervisor from a different department asking you to do something outside your normal job requirements?

How do you answer these questions?

▶ Employers look for honest employees who do not steal or let people steal from them.

▶ They also look for employees who work hard.

▶ Generally, employers want you to talk to your immediate supervisor first, if there are any problems on the job.

▶ Doing anything that goes against company policy is not acceptable.

The job offer is contingent on a clean drug test. I am worried that the medications I take will show up when I go in for drug testing. If they find out that I take medication, I will never get the job.

You can *stop worrying* if the employer uses a testing laboratory and a Medical Review Officer (MRO) service to handle the drug testing. If your test results are positive, the results are sent to the MRO, who will call you for an explanation. That is your opportunity to explain the legally prescribed medications. *The MRO will then report the test as a negative to the employer who will not be informed of your legal medications.*

However, if drug testing is performed at the place of business, at a private doctor's office, or if the employer does not use a MRO service, *it is possible that the employer will find out about the prescription drugs*. The employer may or may not give you a chance to explain your medication usage.

Not all employers handle applicant screening in the same way. Some will be thoughtful and try to accommodate your needs, while others will not.

Regardless of the situation, be truthful when asked about medications. Above all, know your limitations and know the affect those medications have on your ability to properly and safely perform the job for which you are applying. In fact, some employers have a safety policy *requiring* employees to report prescription medications that can cause a safety risk.

The use of illegal drugs or the abuse of legal substances is not protected under the ADA. Drug testing typically screens for narcotics, cocaine, stimulants, marijuana, alcohol, and some prescription medications. *An employer will probably not hire you if illegal drugs are found in your urine.*

> An employer *may not discriminate in hiring you* because you are using prescription drugs.

It is illegal for the laboratory and MRO to release any medical information to current or prospective employers, except to report the presence of illegal drugs or potential safety risks.

Remember, a doctor can disqualify you for the job if the medications that you take would interfere with the job for which you are applying. By law, you cannot be discriminated against if you can perform the essential functions of the job, so be sensible about your job goals.

For example: A truck driver who takes narcotics for pain would be disqualified from driving safety sensitive jobs, such as driving commercial trucks, aircraft operations, and operating commercial boats. which are strictly regulated by the Department of Transportation (DOT) , the Federal Aviation Administration (FAA), and the U.S. Coast Guard.

Coping With Rejection

If I have poor credit or a recent bankruptcy, will I be unable to find a job?

NO: Poor credit usually affects only positions with financial institutions, such as banks, credit authorization companies, collection agencies, insurance companies, or other jobs where handling or managing money or credit is a primary responsibility.

> If you are concerned that your credit rating will affect your hiring, call the prospective employer's human resources department prior to filling out an application. Find out whether or not they can hire someone with credit difficulties.

Some companies will hire people who have certain types of credit problems, like unpaid medical bills, but not other problems, like bankruptcies.

I am in recovery from drug and/or alcohol abuse. Do I have to tell my prospective employer?

Organizations working with drug and/or alcohol addicts may have strict policies regarding sobriety. If you do not disclose the truth during the hiring process, later you can be fired on the spot. Medical professionals, doctors, nurses, and pharmacists will need to consult their licensing and credentialing organizations.

Coping With Rejection (continued)

I have a criminal record. Does that mean I can never get a good job again?

Whether or not you were rejected for a position due to your record depends upon the company's policies, the particular position, the type of crime on your record, how many years it's been since your infraction, and possibly your attitude during the interview when discussing the offense.

Some companies have very strict policies and will not consider hiring anyone with a felony or certain misdemeanors.

Social service agencies may be restricted from hiring people with felonies due to funding regulations.

Jobs involving work with children or the elderly, law enforcement jobs, money handling jobs, and other positions of responsibility usually will not consider someone with a recent felony.

Nonetheless, there remain many companies that will evaluate each applicant, each type of crime, and the length of time since the crime was committed before disqualifying someone due to a criminal record.

Unless you have been convicted of a felony, you need not disclose any criminal background on an application.

Companies vary on how far back they go to conduct a criminal background check. Many companies only consider crimes committed in the last seven to ten years.

Go confidently in the direction of your dreams. Live the life you have imagined.

—Henry David Thoreau

Starting A New Job

Congratulations! You have succeeded in getting hired.

The next step is preparing yourself for working. This chapter will walk you through some of the feelings and challenges that you may face as you start your new job.

Again, you have come a long way. Congratulations!

You Are Going To Start Work. What's Next?

☐ **Do I have my uniform/work clothes ready?**

☐ **Are child-care arrangements in place?**

☐ **Do I know how to get to work?**

☐ **How long does it take to get to work?**

☐ **Can I make it on time? What about a trial run?**

☐ **Do I need reasonable accommodations? If so, what?**

☐ **Have I contacted my support systems to let them know the good news and to allow them to continue to support me through this transition?**

☐ **Smile! You have successfully completed your job search and are ready to go to work now!**

Your First Day At Work

Well, pretty exciting, wasn't it?

Lots of new people, new ideas, machines, and so much to do and learn.

Are you a little tired? Nervous?

Wondering how you did?

 *Check all that apply:*

☐ I got to work on time.

☐ My children were picked up on time.

☐ I was able to get along with my co-workers.

☐ I met some interesting people.

☐ I learned something new.

☐ I earned some money.

☐ I was able to be helpful.

☐ I was productive.

Relax, enjoy. It will get easier and less confusing.

You will get to know your co-workers and build relationships.

You are beginning a new phase of your life!

Resources

Transferable Skills

Among the many excellent resources for identifying your transferable skills and alternative jobs, based on your past work history, are:

Dictionary of Occupational Titles, Revised 4th Edition, (1991), JIST Publishing

The Complete Guide for Occupational Exploration (1993), JIST Publishing

Enhanced Guide for Occupational Exploration (1995)

By looking up your job title in the glossary of the *Dictionary of Occupational Titles,* your can see descriptions of your previous jobs, their typical duties and physical requirements. The *Dictionary of Occupational Titles* also references a GOE (*Guide for Occupational Exploration*) number for each job listed.

The GOE number refers to the chapter in the *Guide for Occupational Exploration* which lists jobs using similar skill sets, and it describes in more detail the physical requirements for the jobs.

Also useful for identifying transferable skills is:

O*Net Dictionary of Occupational Titles (2nd ed., August 2001), JIST Publishing

If you use the O*NET titles to identify jobs, you can utilize the Internet to find out more about these jobs at the Bureau of Labor Statistics web site. **www.bls.gov**

Other career books that may be helpful include:

    Best Jobs for the 21st Century, 2nd Edition

    Best Jobs for the 21st Century for College Graduates

    Enhanced Occupational Outlook Handbook, 3rd Edition (2000) is an excellent resource for researching jobs expected to be in demand in the coming years.

Bibliography

American College Testing Program. (1989). *The DISCOVER Program*. Hunt Valley, MD: Discover Center.

American College Testing Program. (1993). *Realistic Assessment of Vocational Experiences.* Hunt Valley, MD: Discover Center.

Blackwell, T.L., Conrad, A.D., and Weed, R.O. (1992). *Job Analysis and the ADA: A Step-by-Step Guide*. Athens, GA: Elliott & Fitzpatrick, Inc.

Bolles, R. (2003). *What Color is Your Parachute?* Berkeley, CA: Ten Speed Press.

Brown, Dale S. (2000*) Learning a Living, A Guide to Planning Your Career and Finding a Job for People With Learning Disabilities, Attention Deficit Disorder, and Dyslexia,* Woodbine House

Bissonette, D. (1994). *Beyond Traditional Job Development: The Art of Creating Opportunity.* Chatsworth, CA: Milt Wright & Associates.

Bureau of Labor Statistics. (1998). *Occupational Outlook Quarterly.* Washington, DC: U.S. Department of Labor.

Campbell, B., Gosselin, T., and Marrone, J. (1981). *Job-Seeking Skills: Manual and Reference Guide.* KS: Massachusetts Rehabilitation Commission.

Duncan, B., and Woods, D.E. (Eds.). (1989). *Ethical Issues in Disability and Rehabilitation.* New York: World Rehabilitation Fund.

Enright, M., Conyers, L., & Szymanski, E. (1996). "Career and Career-Related Educational Concerns of College Students With Disabilities." *Journal of Counseling and Development, 75,* 103-114.

Farley, R.C., and Bolton, B. (1994). *Developing an Employability Assessment and Planning Program.* Fayetteville: Arkansas Research and Training Center in Vocational Rehabilitation.

Farley, R.C., and Bolton, B. (1994). *Developing an Employability Assessment Program and Planning Program in Rehabilitation and Educational Settings.* Fayetteville, AR: Arkansas Research and Training Center in Vocational Rehabilitation.

Farley, R.C., Little, N.D., Bolton, B., and Chunn, J. (1993). *Employability assessment and planning in rehabilitation and educational settings.* Fayetteville: Arkansas Research and Training Center in Vocational Rehabilitation.

Farr, J.M. (2002). *Seven Steps to Getting a Job Fast.* Indianapolis, IN: JIST.

Farr, J.M. (1991). *The Very Quick Job Search.* Indianapolis, IN: JIST.

Field, T., and Sink, J. (1980). *The Employer's Manual.* Athens, GA: Udare Service Bureau.

Field, T.F., and Norton, L.P. (1992). "*The Americans with Disabilities Act:" Resource Manual for Rehabilitation Consultants.* Athens, GA: Elliott & Fitzpatrick, Inc.

Gatti, I. (1994). "Computer-Assisted Career Counseling: Dilemmas, Problems, and Possible Solutions." *Journal of Counseling and Development, 73,* 51-56.

Good, C.E. (1985). *Does Your Resume Wear Blue Jeans?: The World's Best Book on Resume Preparation and Job-Search Strategy.* Charlottesville, VA: World Store.

Haldane Associates, (2001) *Salary Tips for Professionals*. Impact Publications, Manassas Park, VA.

Half, R. (1981). *The Robert Half Way to Get Hired in Today's Job Market.* New York: Rawson, Wade Publishers, Inc.

Harrington, T.F. (1997). "Career Development Theory" in T.G. Harrington (ed.), *Handbook of Career Planning* (2nd ed., pp. 3-40) Austin, TX: PRO-ED.

Harrington, T.F., and O'Shea, A.J. (1984). *Guide to Occupational Exploration* (2nd ed.). Circle Pines, MN: American Guidance Service.

Harris, M.L., Thompson, B., Fox, M., and Hall, R. (1992). *Reasonable Accommodations at Work: A Guide for Employers*. San Diego, CA: Workable Solutions, Inc.

Holland, J. (1994). *The Self-Directed Search*. San Antonio, TX: Psychological Corp.

Hood, A.B., & Johnson, R.W. (1997). *Assessment in Counseling* (2nd ed.). Alexandria, VA: American Counseling Association.

Isaacson, L.E., & Brown, D. (1997). *Career Information, Career Counseling, and Career Development.* Needham Heights, MA: Allyn & Bacon

Isaacson, L.E. (1986). *Career information in Counseling and Career Development* (4th ed.). Boston: Allyn & Bacon.

Janda, John (2009). *Jobs! For the People Hardest To Serve- 'Ticket To Work' Offenders, Welfare, Homeless, Youth-at-Risk and more.* Academy Press, CA, Santa Ana CA 92705.

Jandt, F.E., & Nemnich, M.B. (1997). *Using the Internet and the World Wide Web in Your Job Search: The Complete Guide to Online Job Seeking and Career Information.* Indianapolis, IN: JIST.

JIST. (1998). *Occupational Information Network.* Indianapolis, IN: JIST Works.

Kalt, N.C. (1996). *Career Power: A Blueprint for Getting the Job You Want.* Pound Ridge, NY: Career Power Books.

Krannich, Ronald L., PH.D, (2002). *No One Will Hire Me!.* Manassas Park, Va: Impact Publications.

Lock, R.D. (1992). *Taking Charge of Your Career Direction* (2nd ed.). Pacific Grove, CA: Brooks/Cole.

Lock, R.D. (2000). *Job Search: Career Planning Guide, Book 2* (4th ed.). Belmont, CA: Wadsworth/ Thomson Learning.

Medley, H.A. (1984). *Sweaty Palms: The Neglected Art of Being Interviewed.* Berkeley, CA: Ten Speed Press.

Mitchell, J.S. (1994). *The College Board Guide to Jobs and Career Planning.* New York: College Entrance Examination Board.

Nester, M. (1994). "Psychometric Testing and Reasonable Accommodations for Persons With Disabilities," in S.M. Bruyere and J. O'Keefe (eds.), *Implications of the Americans With Disabilities Act for Psychology* (pp. 25-35). New York: Springer Publishing Company.

Parker, R.M., and Schaller, J. (1996). "Issues in Vocational Assessment and Disability," in E. Szymanski and R. Parker (eds.), *Work and Disability* (pp. 127-164). Austin, TX: PRO-ED.

Peterson, N., and Gonzalez, R.G. (2000). *The Role of Work in People's Lives: Applied Career Counseling and Vocational Psychology.* Belmont, CA: Wadsworth/Thomson Learning.

Peterson, N., and Gonzalez, R.G. (2000). *Career Counseling Models for Diverse Populations: Hands-On Applications by Practitioners.* Belmont, CA: Wadsworth/Thomson Learning.

Pimentel, R., Bissonette-Lamemdella, D., and Wright, A.L. (1987). *Job Placement for the Industrially Injured Worker.* Chatsworth, CA: Milt Wright & Associates.

Reardon, R.C., Lenz, J.G., Sampson, J.P., and Peterson, G.W. (2000). *Career Development and Planning:A Comprehensive Approach.* Belmont, CA: Wadsworth/Thomson Learning.

Rose, R.G. (1993). *Practical Issues in Employment Testing.* Odessa, FL: Psychological Assessment Resources, Inc.

Rubin, S.E., and Roessler, R.T. (1995). *Foundations of the Vocational Rehabilitation Process* (4th ed.). Austin, TX: PRO-ED.

Savino, Carl S. Major, USAR (Ret.) and Ronald L. Krannich, Ph.D. (2001) *Military Resumes and Cover Letters,* Impact Publications.

Seligman, L. (1994). *Developmental career counseling and assessment* (2nd ed.). Thousand Oaks, CA: SAGE Publications.

Temes, Roberta, Ph.D, (2002) *Getting Your Life Back Together When You Have Schizophrenia.* New Harbinger Publications, Inc.

Thomas, R., Lewis, J.C., and Jensen, N. (1988). *Job Seekers' Guide to Employment.* San Diego, CA: Job Seekers' Publications.

U.S. Department of Labor. (1991). *Dictionary of Occupational Titles* (4th ed., revised). Washington, DC: U.S. Government Printing Office.

Weed, R.O., and Field, T.F. (1994). *Rehabilitation Consultant's Handbook.* Athens, GA: Elliott & Fitzpatrick, Inc.

Zunker, Vernon G., (1994) *Using Assessment Results for Career Development,* Brooks/Cole Publishing Company.